D0102683

DNA in the COURTROOM
A Trial Watcher's Guide

By Howard Coleman
and Eric Swenson

Edited by Dwight Holloway
and Teresa Aulinskas

Published by GeneLex Press
Seattle, Washington USA 1994

DNA in the COURTROOM

A Trial Watcher's Guide

First Edition

Copyright 1994 GeneLex Press

2203 Airport Way South #350
Seattle, Washington 98134 USA

Library of Congress Cataloging-in-Publication Data

Coleman, H. C. (Howard C.) 1940-
Swenson, E. D. (Eric D.) 1942-
DNA in the Courtroom A Trial Watcher's Guide / Howard C. Coleman and Eric D. Swenson.

 p. cm.

includes bibliographical references, glossary and guide to forensic DNA usage by states.

ISBN 09644507-0-4

1. "DNA Fingerprinting." 2. Forensic Science. 3. Scientific Evidence. I. Title

94-073363

Printed in USA

2 3 4 5

DEDICATION

This book is dedicated to the tens of thousands of crime victims and their families who have seen their assailants brought to justice, to the thousands of falsely accused who have been exonerated, and to the hundreds of thousands of children who will grow up knowing who their biological parents are...all with the help of DNA testing.

Table of Contents

CHAPTER FOUR
DNA IN PARENTAGE TESTING

CHAPTER FIVE
DNA IN THE COURTROOM

CHAPTER SIX
PEOPLE V. ORENTHAL JAMES SIMPSON

AFTERWORD

APPENDIX: DNA TESTING IN 50 STATES

GLOSSARY

RECOMMENDED RESOURCES

The DNA Fingerprinting Story (Continued)

On the front page of the New York Times last week there was news of three people incarcerated for rape who are soon to be released because DNA evidence clearly shows that they could not have been the rapists. This follows two other recent reports of the use of DNA technology - to identify the drowned corpse of an infant whose features were unrecognizable, and to resolve a paternity suit in which a child's father accepted financial responsibility when told that DNA evidence of his relation to the child was conclusive. This acceptance of the validity of DNA evidence is exactly what most scientists in this area have believed appropriate, and a rebuke to the judicial process that has been so slow to accept DNA evidence by failing to see that a couple of outspoken individuals were less representative of the scientific community than the vast majority of careful scholars. (It is notable that the scientists prominent in casting doubt on DNA use for the prosecution seem to be nowhere in evidence to cast doubt on its use for defense.)

One note of caution that the doubters raise was correct: the need for careful analyses on well-authenticated samples. But their argument that elaborate state machinery is needed to monitor the work of testing agencies is clearly overkill. Undergraduates are now doing good DNA tests, and their results can easily be checked by standard control samples.

Moreover, the genome project is becoming mechanized so rapidly that soon it may be possible to put a DNA sample in an automated machine with both defense and prosecution acting as witnesses to the procedure. Mutual supervision in an authenticated laboratory seems preferable to a test that could, because of incompetence or malfeasance, be very confusing to a jury. In the scientific laboratory, such a suspicion is easily resolved—by doing the test again. In a law court, the double jeopardy argument might make such a simple solution impossible.

One of the incredible features of the DNA debate is the peculiar standard that some courts try to establish on the admissibility of evidence. In most rape and murder cases there is unlikely to be eyewitness testimony, and in cases when it is available, the events are so traumatic that eyewitness testimony has a good chance of being erroneous. The FBI and Scotland Yard report that one-third of all suspects in rape cases are released before booking because DNA evidence exonerates them. That use alone is an enormous gain for fairness. An individual indicted for a sex crime, but who later proves his innocence, would have the scandal hanging over him for the rest of his life. Twenty-six states now keep DNA data on felons as well as thumbprints and fingerprints. Some judges are continuing to make silly rules indicating they still do not understand the science, but most courts now accept DNA data as routine. The courts need better procedures to validate new technologies rather than allowing an individual judge to establish a precedent or a few scientists to represent a division in the community when the vast majority are not divided.

There is an irony in this new acceptance of DNA fingerprinting. Ink fingerprinting went through the same type of debate, with questions about whether more than one person could have the same print, whether there could be abuse by police, whether there would be care in sample-taking, and so on. Caution is appropriate; unreasonable doubt is not.

The resolution of a scientific procedure in the case of DNA fingerprinting could set the stage for better use of science by society in the future. Statistics would be a good subject for all lawyers to understand. In the United States 37% of the population dies of cancer, so when a suit states that the ingesting of a single pill already approved by the FDA, or a walk under a power line, or the use of a cellular phone, causes cancer, such a suit should be treated with skepticism, not with a full court press.

The community of scientists can, in this case be proud that is has added a new tool for justice - for conviction of the guilty and acquittal of the innocent. It is to be hoped that scientists can also be part of a dialogue with responsible jurists to aid in resolving the problem of admissibility of evidence.

SCIENCE • VOL. 265 • 19 AUGUST 1994   Daniel E. Koshland Jr.

Even though two government studies and such prestigious journals as Science have endorsed the use of DNA in the courtroom, it continues to be opposed by attorneys and their experts.

PREFACE

This book was originally conceived as a fifty-page technical guide for reporters covering the Simpson trial. As we assembled our material and talked with people, it became clear that just providing information on the scientific aspects was not enough, and that more than a media guide was required. In order to understand what is happening with DNA in the courtroom, it is necessary to examine the context and environment in which science and the law meet.

The DNA war is a clash of the different approaches and interests of law and science. It would be difficult to think of two disciplines that have more disparate approaches to seeking the truth. Scientific truth evolves by the building of consensus through peer review and replicating experiments. For the law, truth is less absolute and more relative to the case at hand. Legal truth is achieved through adversarial argument and judgement. The DNA war is a dramatic, hard fought conflict between these two worlds.

In this short book we have tried to provide a brief overview of DNA issues in advance of the Simpson trial. We are simultaneously working on a more comprehensive book, *Silent Witness: DNA, Crime and Justice in America*, which will tell the full story of the DNA war, the people who fight the battles, and the true crime stories that put a human face on forensic science.

Let us emphasize at the start that we strongly believe that DNA testing properly performed belongs in the courtroom. We share this view with the U.S. Congress Office of Technology Assessment, the National Academy of Sciences and the vast majority of scientists in America. The continuing controversy over the admissibility of DNA evidence makes little sense except to the very few people who benefit from continued confusion.

Howard C. Coleman
Eric D. Swenson
Seattle, Washington
December 13, 1994

ACKNOWLEDGEMENTS

We would like to acknowledge the help of forensic scientists, attorneys and law enforcement officials, and others with whom one or both of us have spoken. Individuals who have been especially helpful include Jim Wooley, Ranajit Chakraborty, Kary Mullis, David Kraft, George Clarke, Larry Mueller, Rockne Harmon, Ellen Wijsman, Barry Scheck, Art Harris, Christian Hogan, Jim Crow, Bruce Weir, Susan Herrera, Tim Bradshaw, Fred Leatherman, Randall Libby, Amy Bakken, Mark Prothero, Elizabeth Thompson, George Sensabaugh, Paul Ferrara, Ron Fourney, Carmen Otero, Jack Ballantyne, Eric Buel, John Simich, John Hartman, Roger Kahn, Jim Harrington, George Duncan, Mark Nelson, George Herrin, Chris Tomsey, Victor Weedn, Gerry Schellenberg, Don MacClaren, Susan Narveson, Daniel Koshland, Richard Safferstein, Brian Wraxall, Benjamin Grunbaum, and Bruce Budowle.

Others who helped in producing the book include Brian Lowney, Tom Wahl, Cuong Ong, Allison Garrison, Linda Jorve, Carolyn Anderson, Joyce Blair, Darlene Pulley, Mariann DeTracy, Teresa Johnston, Michael Sherwood, Ann Pace, Fikre Nigusa, Marianne Dawson, Michel Donath, Laura Sandor-Mendoza, Jane Adams, Kathleen Hosfeld, the staff of O1 Publishing, KP Printing, Teresa Aulinskas and Dwight Holloway.

HCC
EDS

Introduction

DNA was discovered in 1868, at about the same time that the Austrian monk Gregor Mendel formulated the laws of heredity, which laid the foundation for the modern science of genetics. A major breakthrough which eventually made possible forensic uses of DNA occurred in the early 1950s when James Watson and Francis Crick solved the puzzle of DNA's structure and precipitated the revolution in molecular biology which followed.

The Bio-Technology Revolution plays a major and ever-expanding role in our life. Medical genetics and gene therapy already have given us tremendous tools to diagnose and treat inherited diseases. With DNA, parentage testing has become a virtually certain procedure. We use DNA to improve animal and vegetable foodstocks, protect endangered species, verify animal pedigrees, detect war crimes and identify human remains.

Many POW-MIA families have had the satisfaction of finally learning the fate of their loved ones through DNA testing of bones recovered in Viet Nam. DNA testing was used to make sure that the correct remains were returned to families following the war with Iraq. After the inferno at the Branch Davidian complex in Waco, Texas, DNA was the only way to con-

---

Characteristics of DNA

- Each person has a unique DNA profile
- Each person's DNA is the same in every cell
- An individual's DNA profile remains the same throughout life
- Most DNA is the same from person to person
- Some DNA varies from person to person

Non-Forensic Uses of DNA Methods

- Genetic and other disease diagnoses
- Rare, endangered and extinct animals research
- Identifying war casualities

---

firm identities from many of the charred remains.

Our knowledge of the past is considerably strengthened by anthropological and paleontological DNA testing. While Jurassic Park-style reincarnations are fantasy, DNA has been extracted from such remnants of ancient life as fossils, prehistoric bones, and mummies. In the past year, Scotland Yard analyzed a skull fragment and confirmed the identity of Russia's last czar. Ironically, a few months later, a contemporary pretender to the Romanoff name and fortune was unmasked by DNA testing. While these are notable uses of the tests, many people believe DNA's most fascinating use is in criminal identification. Certainly no methodology to emerge thus far from the Bio-Technology Revolution has had a greater impact on the public.

The basic techniques of DNA typing were developed and proven in research and medical laboratories long before they were used in the crime lab. But as we try to reach a fair and just result in the trial of O.J. Simpson, where DNA evidence plays such a prominent role, and as we evaluate the use of DNA testing in the criminal justice system, it helps to remember that the first use of DNA in an

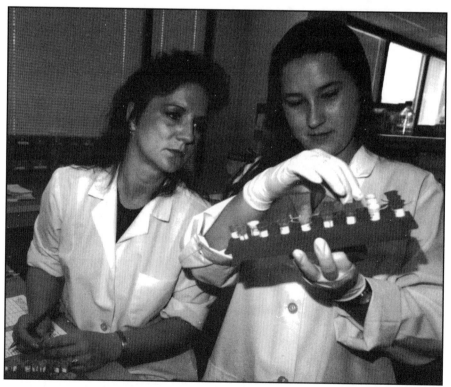

Laboratory personnel inspect and prepare specimens for DNA analysis.

American courtroom occurred only seven short years ago.

Since forensic DNA testing was introduced in 1986, it already has been used in approximately 50,000 criminal investigations in the U.S. alone. DNA evidence is most often found in sexual assaults. About three-fourths of the DNA evidence examined by the FBI and other labs consists of semen specimens. About a third of all FBI tests exonerate wrongfully accused men. A quarter of the tests are inconclusive, and about 40% match the suspect's profile.

Most of the DNA case-work is performed in 50 or so federal, state and local police crime laboratories (approximately 300 are found throughout the U.S.). As a result, DNA testing is often regarded as a prosecution tool. Certainly, when DNA is used in court and reported in the media it almost always is being used to prove the prosecutor's case. However, it is important to remember that thousands of tests are performed annually which eliminate innocent persons as suspects.

DNA Analysis Overview

- Forensic testing (Criminal)
  - ~10,000 cases per year
  - 75% involve sexual assault
- Paternity testing (Civil)
  - ~200,000 cases per year
  - ~130,000 use DNA
- Exclusions equal ~30% of all test results

DNA Identification Applications

- Sexual assault
- Homicide and other violent crimes
- Exculpate wrongly accused suspects
- Identify serial crimes
- Identify human remains
- Sex offender tracking
- Parentage testing

There also are now almost a score of cases in which DNA testing has been used to free previously convicted and incarcerated individuals, some of whom have been in prison for up to twelve years. Another advantage of DNA typing is that it leads to considerable savings in the criminal justice system because suspects confronted with DNA evidence often will plead guilty, thereby saving the considerable costs of a trial.

DNA evidence is a powerful tool for justice to be used by both the prosecution and the defense to benefit us all.

DNA in the Courtroom

Chapter 1

Science Meets the Law: The DNA War

The publication of this book coincides with the beginning of the trial of the century. The People of California versus Orenthal James Simpson combines the celebrity and media circus aspects of the Lindbergh kidnapping case with the science under attack scenario of the Scopes Monkey trial over the teaching of evolution in Tennessee public schools. The celebrity element in the Simpson case is especially fascinating because it involves the suspect instead of the victim. There has never been any trial in history that cuts across as many issues. It covers sex and gender, fame and the media, public opinion and the jury system, race and violence, entertainment and commercialization, even of murder.

Before the start of the actual trial, Simpson's lawyers are putting DNA testing on trial. If DNA loses everyone loses, because forensic DNA testing is such a revolutionary improvement to fairness in the criminal justice system. Every year hundreds of thousands of DNA tests are performed in both forensic and paternity cases. These replace older, often uncertain, testing methods, or help to solve cases where other testing would not have been possible.

Despite the proven value of DNA testing, its reception by the courts can be characterized by the ebb and flow of an ongoing war between prosecutors and defense attorneys and their DNA experts. The blame for this war lies partly with the laboratories which developed and introduced the testing, partly with the contentious and fragmented nature of our legal system, and partly with inaccurate media coverage. The DNA showdown in the Simpson case could be the last major battle in the DNA war or it could be just another skirmish in this expensive and senseless war fought with academic trivia and specious arguments.

Both sides have experienced DNA lawyers to argue their positions and a stable of veteran expert witnesses. Even as the adversaries prepare for battle, the battlefield is shifting with almost weekly court decisions and scientific events that impact the testimony and arguments. It is certain that the pre-trial evidentiary hearing will go on for weeks as both sides commit all their forces to persuading Judge Lance Ito to rule in their favor.

IN THE BEGINNING

The forensic use of DNA started with the work of Alec Jeffreys, a geneticist at the University of Leicester in Britain's Midlands. In 1984, Jeffreys invented the techniques that took human identification from the laboratory to the courtroom. With his co-workers, he also demonstrated that forensic samples, dried stains several years old, contained sufficient DNA to yield conclusive results. Jeffreys proved that even small fragments of DNA molecules were virtually unique to individuals. With appropriate dramatic flair, he called the process he invented "DNA fingerprinting," a term most forensic scientists dislike because it is confusing and can be misleading.

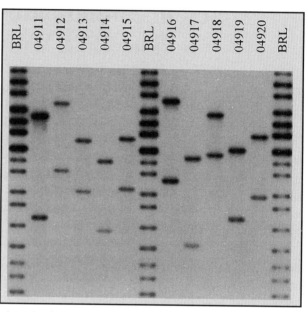

A typical set of DNA profiles produced by the current method of examining one gene at a time (single locus profiling) as opposed to Jeffreys' original method of producing a bar code like (multi locus) profile. Each of the vertical numbered "lanes" with two "bands" contains DNA from a different individual. The lanes with many bands contain calibration standards.

The "fingerprint" produced by the test bears a superficial resemblance to a supermarket bar code with the differences between individuals revealed by the spacing between the 15 or 20 lines called bands. The differences between specimens are measured by a process called Restriction Fragment Length Polymorphism (RFLP) analysis.

Jeffreys' new form of genetic typing and the law were linked from the beginning. He sought high-profile forensic tests for his brainchild. First, he applied it to an immigration case. A boy from Ghana sought to emigrate to Britain, claiming that his mother was already a resident. Conventional blood tests were not conclusive beyond confirming that the two could be related. DNA analysis showed beyond reasonable doubt that the relationship was as claimed, and the Home Office put its stamp of approval on the new technology.

FINDING THE PITCHFORK
IN THE HAYSTACK

A detective in the East Midlands read of the case and sought Jeffreys' help in solving the vicious murder and rape of two British schoolgirls. The police held a prime suspect in the case, a kitchen porter at an insane asylum who had confessed to one of the murders. They brought Jeffreys semen samples from the murder scenes and a blood sample from the suspect. Jeffreys confirmed that the same person committed both crimes but it was not the suspect the police held. On November 21, 1986, the kitchen porter became the first person in the world to have his innocence proven by DNA testing.

Both the police and villagers in the area felt strongly that the killer was someone in their midst. Police were prompted to try something entirely new. All male residents between the ages of 17 and 34 were asked to voluntarily submit a blood sample. Within a month, a thousand men had been "blooded." By May 1987 the number had risen to more than 3,600. Summer turned to Fall, it seemed that this experiment was destined to be as unproductive as the previous, more conventional efforts.

Then the police received an unexpected tip. A bakery manager chatting in a pub with some of her employees learned that one of their colleagues, Colin Pitchfork, had convinced another baker to be blooded in his stead. After four long years and the disappointment of the porter's false confession, the detectives felt this was the break they were looking for. They went to Pitchfork's home and moments after arresting him, he confessed. He became the 4,583rd and last man to be tested in the hunt for the Midlands killer. His sample provided a perfect match to the sperm taken from his two young victims. It was September of 1987 and forensic DNA was on its way.

COMMERCIAL DEVELOPMENT IN THE UNITED STATES

It also was in 1987 that the British firm of Cellmark Diagnostics opened a branch in Germantown, Maryland and introduced Jeffreys' methods in the United States (Cellmark is the private laboratory performing testing for the prosecutor in the Simpson case). The firm is part of Imperial Chemical Industries, a giant British company, which previously established a DNA laboratory in Abingdon, England. When Cellmark set up its operation in this country, it had only one other competitor, Lifecodes Corporation of Valhalla, New York. Founded in 1982, Lifecodes began forensic DNA testing in 1987 and took the lion's share of the market early.

Lifecodes performed the tests in the first case in the United States in which a criminal was identified by DNA. The trial of accused rapist Tommy Lee Andrews began in Orlando, Florida on November 3, 1987. A scientist from Lifecodes and a M.I.T. biologist testified that semen from the victim matched Andrews' DNA, and that Andrews' print would be found in only 1 in 10 billion individuals. On November 6, 1987, the jury returned a guilty verdict and Andrews was subsequently sentenced to 22 years in prison.

This case was heavily reported by the press, creating a media blitz favorable to the new technology. Defense attorneys were caught off guard by the technology and largely accepted it without question. Other cases quickly followed with the same result. Judges and juries were clearly impressed with this new technology.

The introduction of DNA methods to the courtroom by private companies was unique in the history of forensic science. The sharp competition, the proprietary approach of the industry and their desire to keep their products and processes under wraps did not create a favorable environment in which to launch a new technology with such vast potential for changing the criminal justice system. Patent challenges, litigation, and technology-licensing questions became the norm and continue to impede the introduction of technological improvements.

The usual methods of testing new scientific methods are publication and peer review. The requirements for standardization and replication in multiple labs and evaluation of test performance under exacting environmental conditions are of paramount importance in the validation of a forensic test. These did not occur as the commercial laboratories maintained secrecy while rushing to get a return on their substantial investment and start-up costs.

In essence, the major private companies were racing with each other to the courtroom. They hoped to license their procedures and sell their proprietary materials and reagents to as many crime laboratories as they could. They used different tools that produced incompatible results which precluded comparison. As DNA testing became established, some labs were overwhelmed with casework.

Systems were not yet in place to ensure quality control, nor had the labs performed sufficient validation studies. They were run like research labs, having been started by academic scientists, not forensic scientists. While the juggernaut of DNA seemed unstoppable, the very speed with which it was moving boded ill.

RUSH TO JUDGMENT

Case after case involving DNA evidence was won by the prosecution on the basis of testing and testimony provided by Lifecodes and Cellmark. The two companies, while competing for the same business, often joined forces to promote the new technology to the bench, bar, and law enforcement. Their job was made easier by an adulatory press that wrote numerous stories about the miracle technology that fingered criminals with unerring accuracy.

Judges accepted the assertions of industry witnesses at face value and juries were wowed by the big numbers they were offered. In the words of a Massachusetts Supreme Court justice, DNA had acquired an "aura of infallibility." One juror in Queens put it succinctly when he said, "You can't argue with science." Judge Joseph Harris of Albany, N.Y., after sentencing a defendant on a murder and rape charge that hinged on DNA evidence, called it the "single greatest advance in the search for truth since the advent of cross-examination."

The reaction within the defense bar ranged from bemusement to shell shock. One Florida prosecutor commiserated with attorneys representing guilty clients. "If they print your guy with this stuff, you're dead. You can't combat it. There is no defense to it." Defense attorney Robert Brower's assessment was equally unequivocal. He felt that DNA evidence threatened the constitutional right to a fair trial. "In rape cases, when the semen has been matched with the defendant's and the chance that it came from another person is 33 billion to 1, you don't need a jury."

Across the board, the new technology was changing the criminal justice system, and defense attorneys didn't like this development. Of course, they could hope that at least some of the DNA convictions would be reversed on appeal. In the meantime, they were clearly on the defensive as they never had been before.

NEW YORK V. CASTRO: THE CHINK IN THE ARMOR

When police arrived at the Bronx apartment of Jeffrey Otero in February 1987, they discovered a scene of terrible carnage. Vilma Ponce, Otero's seven months pregnant common-law wife, lay on the living room floor, nude from the waist down. She was perforated by more than sixty knife wounds. In the bathroom, police found the body of her two-year-old daughter, Natasha, also repeatedly stabbed.

Police interviewed Jose Castro, the janitor of a neighboring building who fit Otero's description of the suspect. The detective noticed what he thought might be a dried bloodstain on Castro's watch and asked if he could retain it for examination. Shortly thereafter, Castro was arrested and charged with the double murder. The dried blood on Jose Castro's watch and how it was handled led to the first notable courtroom challenge to DNA typing.

Police turned the watch, along with blood samples from Castro and the two victims, over to the Lifecodes Corporation. Scientists analyzed the dried blood and during the 15 week long pre-trial evidentiary hearing, testified that the DNA from the stain matched that of Vilma Ponce, and that the frequency of her patterns in the Hispanic population were 1:189,200,000.

The defense undertook a thorough examination of the genetic analyses and mounted the first extended (and eventually successful) effort to have DNA evidence excluded. What also occurred in the Castro case that contributed to this turn of events was an unprecedented out-of-court meeting between two defense and two prosecution scientific witnesses after they had testified. These scientists all agreed that Lifecodes had failed to use generally accepted scientific techniques in reaching their results matching the blood found on Castro's watch with that of Vilma Ponce. The quality of the data they produced was poor and they did not even follow their own procedures for interpreting the data.

One key player in this drama was Eric Lander, an academician who received his doctorate in mathematics from Oxford University and now directed a genetics research institute at the Massachusetts Institute of Technology. Lander is a powerful personality. Even his friends admit that Lander is arrogant, just as his enemies concede that he is brilliant.

As a result of the testimony of Lander *et al*, the judge ruled that the inclusionary tests suggesting that Ponce was the source of the blood stain were inadmissible, while allowing the exclusionary evidence that the blood did not come from Castro. After almost one hundred cases where DNA evidence met little or no resistance and never was ruled inadmissible, the defense obtained their first victory. Later that year, in what was to be the anti-climax to the case, Castro confessed to the murders, admitting that the blood on his watch came from Vilma Ponce, and pled guilty.

THE FBI AND MOUNTIES RIDE TO THE RESCUE

Fortunately, the Federal Bureau of Investigation and the Royal Canadian Mounted Police entered the picture at about this time, with a salutary effect. The FBI saw the potential for the forensic use of DNA testing at about the same time that Alec Jeffreys was conducting his breakthrough experiments. Along with the National Institutes of Health, the FBI began collaborative research and in 1987, set up its own research unit to establish DNA identification techniques for the Bureau. After one year of testing, ending in late 1988, the FBI set up their own DNA laboratory at their Pennsylvania Avenue headquarters. The RCMP soon followed with their own DNA laboratory.

The Bureau benefitted from the experience of DNA lab pioneers here and in Europe, and was not locked into a single technology or product. When the FBI lab went on-line, it used a combination of four different DNA probes, including those developed by GeneLex, Dr. Raymond White of the Howard Hughes Medical Center, Lifecodes, and Cellmark. DNA probes and primers are the key patented biochemicals used to identify individual genetic differences.

The main result of the FBI and RCMP beginning their own DNA testing was standardization of a chaotic industry. The Federal agency established detailed laboratory protocols, performed appropriate validation studies, and cut through the competing systems, methods, and tools to establish a standardized system that is used in almost all North American laboratories today. The raising of standards became easier once standardization was achieved.

DEFENSE BAR STRATEGY

As a result of the evidentiary hearing in the Castro case, the National Association of Criminal Defense Lawyers (NACDL) set up a DNA Task Force in the Fall of 1989. The new group was headed by Castro's (and now O.J. Simpson's) DNA defense team, Barry Scheck, a professor at Benjamin N. Cardozo Law School, and Peter Neufeld, a private attorney in Manhattan. They asserted that the evidence introduced in the Castro case did more than prove that the DNA industry was fallible. They felt it was simply a case of "the emperor having no clothes." As O.J. Simpson's DNA attorneys they will continue their crusade against DNA, having already filed a more than one hundred page motion to exclude all DNA testing evidence from the trial.

Time has shown that Castro provided a needed psychological boost to defense attorneys and cannon fodder for DNA critics, but otherwise had very little effect on the legal system. The prosecution rendered the key opinion of the trial court moot by agreeing that some of the evidence was inadmissible. Since Castro pled guilty, there was no review on appeal. At the time, however, at least to hopeful commentators, Castro looked like a Waterloo for Lifecodes and the prosecutors who depended on the services of that and similar labs.

The task force announced that its first effort would be to try to reopen all convictions involving evidence tested by Lifecodes. Neufeld even suggested that the thousands of court orders in paternity suits decided by DNA testing also were of questionable validity because of the signal victory in Castro.

While this wholesale repudiation of DNA testing has remained an unrealized dream, NACDL's DNA task force has been a large factor in the DNA war, by leveling the playing field, escalating the conflict, and keeping the conflict alive against all odds. Part of their catching up with the competition consisted of taking the offensive and mounting a public relations campaign. Some of the press printed new articles which were as critical of DNA typing as previous accounts had been enthusiastic.

UNITED STATES V. YEE

In the Spring of 1990, Scheck and Neufeld began to prepare for a trial in Ohio, United States vs. Yee, that would be a rigorous judicial inquiry into the soundness of DNA testing.

Three members of the Cleveland chapter of the Hell's Angels motorcycle gang, Steven Yee, Mark Verdi, and John Bonds, were accused of killing David Hartlaub of Sandusky, Ohio. The defendants allegedly killed Hartlaub because they mistakenly thought him to be a member of the rival Outlaw's Motorcycle Club, with whom they were having a turf war. The victim was shot fourteen times with a silenced MAC 10 machine gun inside his own van.

Most of the blood was later determined to be Hartlaub's, but blood typing tests revealed that some was not. Detectives theorized that a ricocheting bullet had hit one of the suspects. DNA analysis by the FBI showed a match between blood from the van, from Yee's car, and from John Bonds. It was this evidence that the defense planned to challenge.

In a way, Castro was a dress rehearsal for Yee. Many of the rising stars in the DNA constellation appeared as witnesses for one side or the other at the June 1990 hearing in Toledo before U.S. Magistrate James Carr. The prosecutor called six witnesses; including Thomas Caskey of the Baylor College of Medicine, who had just finished serving as head of a panel that examined forensic DNA for the Congressional Office of Technology Assessment; Kenneth Kidd, a Yale geneticist; and Bruce Budowle, the FBI's main DNA scientist. The defense had five experts including Richard Lewontin, and Daniel Hartl, geneticists at Harvard and Washington University, respectively. The court called Eric Lander, the M.I.T. mathematician-turned-geneticist who had testified in Castro.

The defense launched a full-scale attack on the FBI and its work. They claimed that the Bureau's published articles on its matching criteria were ambiguous or inconsistent and sought access to the supporting data. The prosecutor fought the motion for discovery, but the court granted the defense access to these materials. The experts pored over the data and had a field day, citing what they claimed to be errors, omissions, lack of controls, and faulty analysis.

James Wooley, the federal prosecutor, countered the criticism by reiterating two telling points. First, regardless of disputes over match criteria, the multi-probe match produced by the FBI was highly unlikely if specimens came from two different people. Hence the chance of an innocent person being incriminated was virtually nil. Second, (and the court noted that there were "troublesome questions about the quality of the Bureau's work"), whatever deficiencies existed went to the weight not the admissibility of the evidence. The magistrate concurred and the DNA matches were admitted. They also were admitted at the homicide trial in state court and passed muster on appeal.

Barry Scheck considered the Yee case to be far more significant than Castro to the defense bar. The documents procured from the FBI and others through the discovery process were to find their way into many courtrooms throughout the land. While they had lost the battle at Toledo, Scheck, Neufeld, and their cohorts had seized reams of ammunition and gained new recruits for the many battles that lay ahead.

GOOD INTENTIONS BACKFIRE: THE NRC REPORT

Just after the Congressional Office of Technology Assessment published a report recommending the continued use of forensic DNA in 1989, a second federal study was initiated in response to "a crescendo of questions." Funding was procured for a more definitive study of the problems, this time by the National Academy of Science's National Research Council (NRC). One of the deans of American genetics, Victor McKusick, was picked to chair the fourteen person panel. They began their work in January 1990.

From the beginning, the courtroom battles over DNA were refought in the National Academy of Sciences committee rooms, and with nearly the same ferocity. The most contentious issue was the matter of how to calculate statistical probability, the odds that a match between DNA found at the crime crime and DNA taken from the suspect could be the result of coincidence. To find a match, crime labs look at several sites where the DNA is known to vary. If these sites match, there is an extremely high probability that the samples came from the same person. To quantify these findings, investigators calculate the frequency with which each variation occurs in the suspect's population group. The frequencies for each site are then multiplied together to arrive at a figure for the complete DNA profile.

Databases of DNA profiles for various populations have been gathered for use in making these calculations.

To some population geneticists, there's the rub. Friction over this point provided the spark that was fanned by the theory of the two geneticists, Richard Lewontin and Daniel Hartl. They maintained that the frequencies of genetic markers in sub-groups could differ widely from the frequencies found in larger population groups. If this is so, then any estimates calculated using the widely accepted FBI match-binning methods could be considerably wide of the mark. Proponents of this theory insisted that extensive and expensive population studies must be completed before reliable estimates could be introduced into the courtroom, even if this takes a decade or more. While Eric Lander didn't go all the way down this road, he was a fellow traveler enough of the distance to become the champion of extreme caution, representing the extreme view on the panel.

NRC Report

- Proposes Ceiling Principle
- No population geneticists or statisticians on panel
- Suggested studies were unsound
- Internally inconsistent
- Does not address paternity or PCR
- Growing body of papers refute NRC report
- NRC has convened new panel

At the other end was Thomas Caskey, then president of the American Society of Human Genetics, an advisor to the FBI, and developer of technology used in DNA analysis. Caskey took the widely predominant view that while population subgroups do exist, current methods of calculation were so conservative that they would compensate for such variations and actually already favored the suspect. While Lewontin and Hartl's ideas might have a legitimate place in academic discussions, the pragmatists argued that they didn't belong in the courtroom because even if they were sound, the chance of a false match was negligible. Nevertheless a compromise was struck and called the interim ceiling principle. It was a clearcut effort to design a standard so biased in favor of the defendant that all sides would accept it.

The committee's report, *DNA Technology in Forensic Science*, was released in mid-April 1992. It endorsed the continued use of DNA typing in the courts, pushed for standardization, mandatory accreditation and proficiency testing for DNA labs, and called for an expert committee that would provide oversight and advisory assistance. The committee hoped their work might write a finish to the costly pre-trial hearings and inconsistent rulings that were increasingly the result when DNA evidence was introduced.

They didn't have to wait long to be proven wrong. Critics such as Peter Neufeld howled "foul." They claimed there was an inherent bias to the project because it had been largely funded by the Department of Justice, which had a stake in its outcome. They cited the lengthy criticism of the statistics chapter by the FBI as undue pressure. They charged Thomas Caskey, who had resigned from the panel a few months before it released its report, with conflict of interest since he had proprietary interests in DNA technology. But they saved their harshest criticism for "the interim ceiling principle," which they found to be a hodge-podge of elements combined for the express purpose of forging consensus. Interestingly enough many forensic scientists agreed with them on this point.

While criticism from the defense bar and their academic supporters certainly should have been expected, the response from some in law enforcement and others who favored DNA typing was not. The FBI held a press conference upon release of the report. John Hicks did say that the Bureau was pleased with the study, but when asked directly, refused to endorse it. There was much in the report, such as accreditation by an outside agency, that ran counter to the FBI ethos. Others felt that the interim ceiling principle went too far in favoring the criminal. Before long, a flurry of papers attacking the panel's solution as flawed, just plain bad science, appeared. And no wonder. The committee was opining on matters of statistics and population genetics, but nobody on the panel had a background in either field. The defense bar stood back and guffawed at the unintended support they were receiving from unexpected quarters.

In retrospect, the committee's hope that its report would be the final word on the subject seems pathetically naive. Every competent defense lawyer in the country now cites the NRC report in arguing for the exclusion of DNA evidence. There is considerable irony in how this attempt to clarify the waters surrounding DNA led to muddying them instead. The National Academy of Sciences' effort stands as a textbook example of good intentions gone awry.

THE MEDIA AND DNA

Having looked at the DNA war and how it is fought in the courts, and to some extent in academia, let us consider how it is presented to the court of public opinion by the media. Early on, the press was part of the DNA juggernaut. It proclaimed the new technology to be a miracle, if not infallible, and glowingly recorded its victories. Later, some of the press seemed eager to atone for this early, unqualified endorsement by giving the opponents of DNA testing free rein to air their objections and charges, several of which are both unfounded and unchallenged.

New questions swirl around DNA testing

By Ordway P. Burden

It is a wise man who remembers Ben Franklin's comment that nothing is certain in this world but death and taxes.

Take DNA "fingerprinting," for example. A year ago. DNA fingerprint...

Restriction Fragment Length Polymorphism (RFLP)
Multi & Single Locus DNA Probes

than 500 rape and homicide cases.

"The crime scene evidence was matched with the primary suspect in 43 percent of those cases," he said. "Perhaps more significant, in 23 percent of those cases, the primary sus...

NEWS 8   The Orange County Register   FOCUS: THE SIMPSON CASE Wednesday, Oct. 12, 1994

DNA: NOT THE MAGIC BULLET?

items, Superior Court Judge Lance Ito said he might exclude

Some Scientists Doubt the Value Of 'Genetic Fingerprint' Evidence

Simpson case may set DNA precedent

Expert says splitting blood samples for tests is high-stakes question

By LINDA DEUTSCH
Associated Press

DNA test results show a match between Simpson's blood and blood drops found near the bodies of Simpson's ex-wife and her friend.

Simpson's attorneys contend many of the samples are too tainted to be used a trial because they have been mislabeled, mishandled and contaminated. But they want to conduct their own tests anyway.

Simpson, 47, has pleaded no guilty to charges he murdered Nicole Brown Simpson and Ronald Goldman June 12 outside his ex-wife's condominium.

In other developments:
● Simpson's attorneys claimed yesterday that District Attorney Gil...

O.J. Simpson

DNA 'fingerprints' not valid yet

FORENSICS: Genetic testing is not ready for the courts, UCI expert says.

related samples is 1 in several hundred billion.

But other scientists say the chances of a false match are much higher – especially if the possibility of misinterpretation and laboratory error is added in.

son said, DNA evidence just shouldn't be in the courts.

It would be tantamount to bringing forward a witness who positively identifies the killer but when asked how sure he is, says he doesn't know.

Fight Erupts Over DNA Fingerprinting

A bitter debate is raging over how the results of this new forensic technique are interpreted in court

WHEN DNA FINGERPRINTING WAS FIRST introduced in U.S. courts in a 1988 rape case in Florida, it was heralded as a tool of stunning precision, the greatest forensic advance since the advent of fingerprinting itself. After all,

argument appears, Lewontin and Hartl's article will persuade judges to throw DNA evidence out of court and derail the prosecution in numerous cases. It is not an entirely idle fear; already, after hearing testimony

Compelling evidence. *Bands indicate that blood on a defendant's shirt came from the victim (V), not from the defendant. D*

Simpson case is focusing on DNA

Simpson
CONTINUED FROM PAGE 1

Scientific experts have differed on how to interpret DNA tests, so prosecutors must persuade Judge Lance Ito to admit their results. They also must say what the odds are that the blood came from Simpson and not someone else.

Although DNA evidence commonly makes it into California's trial courts, prosecutors depending on it have run into obstacles with some state appellate judges.

Deoxyribonucleic acid is the chemical compound encased in the chromosomes of every human cell that contains the individual's genetic program. Tests compare DNA fragments from hair, body fluid or tissue samples at a crime scene with the DNA of suspects and victims.

Prosecutors and defense lawyers agree that obvious differences in segments of DNA can eliminate a suspect. But they disagree about the reliability of tests in making a positive identification.

If segments from a crime scene match segments from a suspect, scientists use population statistics to estimate the chance that the DNA could have come from more than one person. The chance can range from one in a few thousand to one in billions, depending on the number of segments tested and the mathematics used.

A form of DNA testing — Restriction Fragment Length Polymorphism (RFLP) analysis — is accepted by scientists. But at least two California appeals court judges have thrown the tests out after experts disagreed on how to interpret results. Neither of those appellate rulings reversed verdicts.

Prosecutors said one kind of DNA testing, called PCR, on two samples from the blood trail showed matches with Simpson's blood. One of the samples also underwent RFLP testing, and those results also showed a match with Simpson's blood.

The RFLP test is based on the position of dark bands of DNA taken from crime-scene body fluids or tissue samples appear at the same distance from the top of the film as bands from a suspect's DNA. Once a match is generated, scientists use statistics to help explain how many people might share the pattern.

The media have been a source of information, misinformation, and even disinformation about forensic DNA testing.

There hardly appears any story about DNA, forensic or otherwise, which does not contain some error, significant or not. No doubt part of the problem derives from the difficulties inherent in journalism, the imperative of deadlines; the challenge of comprehending a difficult subject, conveying technical information to a lay audience, etc. The failure of the press to consistently report accurately, and sometimes even fairly, about DNA raises disturbing questions. One that stretches from the press box to the jury box is: if a reporter, with the ability to research a topic and question sources directly can't get DNA right, what can be expected of a typical juror?

NEW YORK TIMES

While numerous instances could be cited to show how the media gets the facts wrong, sensationalizes DNA, or fuels the controversy over it, let us look at one significant example, this one from the *New York Times*.

Perhaps the worst reporting by the *Times* was its reporting of *DNA Technology in Forensic Science*, the report issued by the National Research Council in April 1992. The report strongly endorsed the continued use of DNA typing in the courts.

The *New York Times'* front page article on the findings of the National Research Council was headlined U.S. PANEL SEEKING RESTRICTION ON USE OF DNA IN COURTS. The sub-head read "Judges are Asked to Bar Genetic 'Fingerprinting' Until Basis in Science is Stronger." The article by Gina Kolata began, "A long-awaited Federal report on a powerful new genetic technique for identifying criminal suspects says it should not be allowed in court in the future unless a more scientific basis is established." None of these statements was true.

The reaction to the *Times* reporting on the study was immediate. The chairman of the committee, Victor McKusick of Johns Hopkins, one of the deans of American genetics, felt compelled to call a press conference the day the *Times* article appeared to correct its misrepresentations. Since the *Times* also had ignored the press embargo requested by the DNA Committee, McKusick released the report two days early. The NRC then took the unprecedented step of prefacing their later publication of the study with the following statement:

> On April 14, 1992, the New York Times printed an article on this report. That article seriously misrepresented the findings of this committee; in an article on April 15, the Times corrected the misrepresentation. To avoid any potential confusion engendered by the April 14 article, the committee provides the following clarifying statement:

> We recommend that the use of DNA analysis for forensic purposes, including the resolution of both criminal and civil cases, be continued

while improvements and changes suggested in this report are being made. There is no need for a general moratorium on the use of the results of DNA typing either in investigation or in the courts.

No other paper in the country, save those who relied on the *Times* for their coverage, blew the story. The *Washington Post*, for example, appropriately headed their article, "Panel Backs DNA Tests as Crime Evidence." Unfortunately, there are many papers in the country who count on the *Times*, and news stories and editorials that responded to what was printed in our "national paper of record" spread its misinformation.

This example demonstrates remarkable journalistic incompetence or worse. If this is how one of the world's best newspapers reports on DNA testing, it should be no surprise when other media also fail at the task.

BACK TO NATURE

The pre-eminent British journal *Nature* was the first publication to explore forensic DNA. Indeed, it was in Nature that Alec Jeffreys announced his invention to a wide-circulation audience. Shortly thereafter, the two Home Office scientists who developed Alec Jeffreys' techniques for forensic use published their findings in *Nature*. Since then, this journal has been quick to report developments in the technology and the political twists and turns of the DNA debate.

The most recent twist brought two former opponents, Bruce Budowle of the FBI and Eric Lander of MIT, into agreement. They co-authored an article entitled "DNA fingerprinting dispute laid to rest" in the October 27, 1994 issue of *Nature*. Budowle was a principle architect of the FBI's DNA typing program and Lander was forensic DNA's foremost critic, serving as a witness in both the Castro and Yee cases and as a vocal member of the National Research Council committee.

Several defense attorneys and witnesses who still oppose the use of DNA testing by the prosecution immediately charged that Lander and Budowle were trying to influence Judge Lance Ito who is presiding over the Simpson case. Neither expert denied that this was their intention. Indeed, both the timing and content of the article confirm this aim. These experts fear that for attorneys, whose primary roles are adversarial, to prepare "the most detailed course in molecular genetics ever taught to the U.S. people," the "likely result is confusion." They anticipate that the media is preparing for this result with warnings that DNA fingerprinting remains controversial and plagued by unresolved technical issues.

For his part, Lander seems to have recognized that he has added to the confusion over DNA and wants to rectify his previous actions. He also is satisfied that laboratory quality assurance has been achieved and that the population genetics debate is settled. Budowle, who believes that the interim ceiling principle is far too conservative a way to estimate genetic profile frequencies, concedes that even if that standard is weighted too much in the defendant's favor, it is better than having a more realistic standard which would not be accepted by all courts.

Lander and Budowle declare that after 400 technical papers, 100 scientific conferences, three sets of DNA analysis guidelines, 150 court cases, and an exhaustive three-year study by the National Research Council, enough is enough. "The DNA fingerprinting wars are over." Of course, the courts will have the final say and it is clear that the defense bar is not yet willing to sign any treaties. Nevertheless, these two former adversaries are doing their best to cut through the rhetoric and false charges and assure DNA's rightful standing in the courts.

The *Nature* article considers and disposes of several objections to forensic DNA focusing on population genetics, the issue "most often said to remain problematical." It lays the blame for any lingering debate on the subject on the flaws, miswordings, ambiguities, and errors of the original NRC report, especially the recommended interim ceiling principle. Lander and Budowle write that the report failed to state clearly enough that the principle was intended as an "ultra-conservative calculation," a "practical way to sidestep a contentious and unproductive debate," which should not have barred experts from offering their own best estimates of genotype frequency.

The authors are not hopeful that a new NRC report will improve the current situation. They fear that it will give attorneys "new opportunities for misunderstanding." The fact that a new study is in the works has provided the Simpson defense team with the argument that all DNA evidence should be ruled inadmissible until the new report is issued.

Budowle and Lander conclude their article by saying:

> Most of all, the public needs to understand that the DNA fingerprinting controversy has been resolved. There is no scientific reason to doubt the accuracy of forensic DNA typing results, providing that the testing laboratory and the specific tests are on a par with currently practiced standards in the field. The scientific debates served a salutary purpose: standards were professionalized and research stimulated. But now it is time to move on.

THE SECOND TIME AROUND: NRC II

Aghast at the misinterpretations and misuses that have befallen the first National Research Council report, the National Academy of Sciences has convened a second panel to make a scientific assessment of forensic DNA testing. The goal of the committee, already popularly referred to as NRC II, is to update DNA Technology in Forensic Science. To quote from the official statement of task:

The study will emphasize statistical and population genetics issues in the use of DNA evidence. The committee will review relevant studies and data, especially those that have accumulated since the previous report. It will seek input from appropriate experts, including those in the legal and forensics community, and will encourage the submission of evidence from the courts. Among the issues examined will be the extent of population subdivision and the degree to which this information can or should be taken into account in the calculation of probabilities or likelihood ratios. The committee will review and explain the major alternative approaches to the statistical evaluation of DNA evidence, along with their assumptions, merits, and limitations. It will also specifically rectify those statements regarding statistical and population genetics issues in the previous report that have been seriously misinterpreted or led to unintended procedures.

To chair the committee, the National Research Council chose James Crow, a distinguished human geneticist and professor emeritus at the University of Wisconsin. The other ten members of the committee include three law professors, two professors of statistics from Stanford and the University of Chicago, a professor of ecology and evolution, the director of a molecular genetics institute, two physicians who are also geneticists, and a professor of forensic science. While this is unquestionably a "blue ribbon panel," it also appears to be capable of doing what is necessary to clarify the issues and help the courts.

The Committee held its first meeting in the summer of 1994 and plans to hold three more before concluding its work in the summer of 1995. At a public meeting in Washington on November 18, 1994, the committee listened to the advice of experts from the U.S. and Great Britain on the best course to take. It also heard from four invited speakers, three of whom - Ranajit Chakraborty, Elizabeth Thompson, and Lawrence Mueller - will testify in the Simpson trial. The consensus recommendation: keep the report short and simple and produce it quickly. Many in the audience feared that any other type of report would lend itself to continued misapplication by defense attorneys and witnesses who wish to keep the controversy going.

STAKES AND STAKEHOLDERS IN THE DNA WAR

As the DNA war has heated up, there has been a tendency for each side to demonize the other. It is easy for the prosecution to adopt a bunker mentality when under attack while doing their job of protecting us from criminals. The defense bar, largely public defenders, feels under siege because they have even fewer resources than does the prosecution. It also is easy to forget that the defense

History of the DNA War

1984 Alec Jeffreys invents "DNA Fingerprinting"
Kary Mullis invents the PCR method

1986 First PCR case done in US. Pennsylvania v Pestinikas homicide case involving allegations of switching of body parts at a funeral home.

1987 First US Case by the more common RFLP method. Florida v Andrew rape case. Defense caught off guard and helpless.

1989 The FBI and RCMP begin performing DNA testing in their headquarters laboratories.

1990 New York v. Castro double homicide. The Defense unmasks shoddy laboratory work that touches off the DNA wars.

1991 The New York Times begins heavily biased and ongoing reporting on forensic DNA testing.

1991 United States v. Yee homicide tried in Cincinnati Ohio. The first major showdown case over the soundness of the testing methods. After a fifteen week hearing the judge accepted DNA testing.

1992 The National Research Council issues a report on DNA testing intended to endorse the technology, but so poorly executed that it becomes the "bible" for defense attorneys fighting the admissibility of DNA testing.

1993 The United Supreme Court decision in Daubert v. Merrill Dow relaxes admissibility for scientific evidence. No impact on Simpson because of October 1994 California Supreme Court decision in Leahy affirming older Frye standard for admissibility.

1994 The National Research Council reconvenes a committee to try and rectify the harm done by their first report.

1994 The trial of the century. Dollars v. DNA and California v. OJ Simpson.

bar, under our adversarial system, protects us all from overzealous police and prosecutors. On the fringes of the criminal defense bar are those who believe that the state has too much power and that the system is so over balanced in favor of the prosecution that anything that empowers the state is to be fought. This politicization of the judicial process underlies the contention that DNA testing only should be used to exonerate, but not convict an accused.

Even the most articulate critics of DNA typing concede that it is the most powerful tool yet devised for identifying criminals. Most of those involved in court cases find that the current judicial methods of evaluating new technological evidence are inadequate and inappropriate. Costly, long admissibility hearings serve little real purpose except to spend public money and time.

It is tempting to put much of the blame for this situation upon defense attorneys. No less an authority than Alan Dershowitz, the convicted defendant's dream counsel and a member of the Simpson team observed: "The defendant wants to hide the truth because he is generally guilty. The defense attorney's job is to make sure the jury does not arrive at that truth." When defense attorneys challenge evidence presented by the prosecution, they only are doing their job. The defense mounts many arguments and uses various experts in defending its clients. Some are real, others spurious. The defender's obligation is to the defendant, to use all legal means to win his acquittal. While the defense bar bears some responsibility for confusion in the courts and among the public about DNA, it doesn't bear the entire onus.

There is plenty of blame to allocate for causing confusion about DNA. To summarize:

- Forensic DNA testing was developed rapidly and by short-sighted com-mercial interests, the first time a major forensic technology had been introduced by the private sector. One result was that standards were not developed as quickly as they should have been;
- Prosecution witnesses oversold DNA evidence, claiming that the probability of a random match was as low as 1:738,000,000,000,000, creating false expectations about the technology and stacking the odds against the defendant;
- Overeager and hardnosed prosecutors urged these exaggerated figures and denied or delayed legitimate defense requests, exacerbating the inherently adversarial American legal system;
- Expert witnesses, often deriving the bulk of their income from witness fees, have a vested interest in making sure the controversy continues so that they can keep testifying;
- Inaccurate media that thrives on the sensational and the controversial has spread misinformation and disinformation about DNA;
- The judiciary is not always judicious, and is sometimes indifferent to the choices it could exercise to more speedily and certainly strive for justice.

Almost all of us have a stake in clearing up the confusion over forensic DNA. Defense attorneys, their clients, and the expert witnesses they employ are the only ones who benefit from continuing the controversy over DNA.

Chapter 2

DNA as Evidence

THE DAWN OF FORENSIC SEROLOGY

Ever since the early 1900s when Karl Landsteiner discovered the A,B, and O blood types, it has been the dream of forensic serologists (scientists who study body fluids) to be able to positively identify the individual source of a small blood stain. Advances were made during the 1930s in discovering new blood types such as the Rh factor and again in the 1970s with the invention of electrophoresis, a new method for separating and identifying some of the variable proteins found in blood that are the keys to classic genetic typing. Proteins comprise the majority of the structural and functional substances that make up our bodies. Application of more and more of these typing systems allowed an increasing percentage of the wrongly suspected individuals to be excluded as the source of an evidence stain.

A major problem with the classical systems that test proteins found in blood, is that very few of these proteins are also found in semen and other body fluids. Because the majority of cases that require genetic typing are sexual assaults, the lack of a definitive set of useful genetic markers in semen has long been a great handicap to the scientific analysis of rape evidence.

DNA is found in almost every cell in the body. DNA typing has greatly expanded the sources of evidence that can be tested, while simultaneously reducing the amount of evidence necessary to perform a conclusive test.

SOURCES OF DNA FOR TESTING

BLOOD

The surface or substrate on which a bloodstain is found can profoundly affect the ability to successfully perform an analysis. Extracting DNA from dried blood found on glass, metal, hard plastics or lightweight cloth is straightforward.

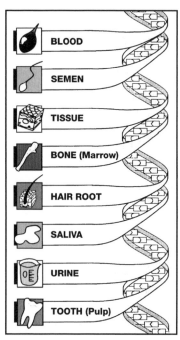

Denim, vinyl, carpet, automobile seats and other dense and heavily colored fibers require additional steps. They often contain substances that inhibit the DNA testing process and which must be removed by a variety of purification methods. Concrete and other similar porous surfaces are difficult simply because it is difficult to separate the blood from the concrete. Soil is an almost impossible substrate from which to obtain usable DNA because current extraction methods are not capable of releasing the DNA from soil.

Blood stains may be mixtures of blood from two different people and can produce DNA profiles that are more complex than those from a single individual. DNA profiling may be the only way to determine if a given stain is a mixture. DNA testing can also determine if specimens are from individuals of a different sex. Gender is the only physical characteristic that can be determined by forensic DNA analysis.

(Office of Technology Assessment Illustration)

Sources of DNA for testing.

Specimens drawn from suspects or victims are called known exemplars and usually consist of liquid blood. The simplest and most reliable samples to work up are liquid whole blood. While the best storage method for blood is frozen, DNA has been successfully isolated after refrigeration for several months. The most common way in which forensic blood samples are handled, following collection, is as a series of dime-sized stains on washed cotton sheeting. This method makes for convenient transport and storage of large numbers of samples.

Occasionally buccal (inside cheek) swabs are supplied as exemplars. All U.S armed forces recruits give both blood and buccal cell samples. This process has the advantage of being non-invasive. It can be used with infants to determine paternity and with other individuals who cannot have blood drawn for medical or religious reasons.

Exemplars may also be obtained from the "Guthrie Cards," widely collected at birth for newborn screening of genetic disease and saved by many states. These have been used in body identification. Similarly a seventeen-year-old band-aid was used to determine the paternity of a young man killed in a car wreck. The question of paternity came up after he was buried, as part of a dispute over insurance benefits.

SEMEN

Semen stains are the most common evidence to be submitted for DNA analysis and are typically examined and tested by conventional methods prior to DNA analysis. Sperm cell specific staining and microscopy help determine if a stain is the result of vaginal drainage. Vaginal swabs or stains resulting from post-coital drainage will typically contain sperm cells mixed with vaginal cells. Sperm cells as dried stains on furniture or clothing may be identifiable for years.

Semen and condoms are surprisingly common in many environments. Identification of one or a few sperm cells, for example, is not considered highly probative. Sexually active women will often have sperm present in the vagina for 72 or more hours following intercourse. That is why it is important to also test the boyfriend or consenting sexual partner of rape victims.

> **Preservation of Evidence**
> - Air dry (no heat) all stains and swabs
> - Store frozen in paper bags, not plastic
> - Tissues store frozen preferably without preservatives (formalin or embalming fluid)
> - Liquid blood refrigerate up to a few weeks (longer term, freeze for DNA testing)

Mixtures of cells are usually a confounding factor when performing standard blood typing. In the case of DNA analysis, the process of differential lysis (a controlled disintegration of the cells), is used to separate the sperm cells or male fraction from the non-sperm cells, "the female fraction."

TISSUES

Isolation of DNA from tissues taken at autopsy is a simple, straightforward process. More often, soft tissues received in the laboratory are from partially decomposed bodies. DNA survival times are low in soft tissues such as liver and kidney, longer in muscle and brain, and longest yet in dense bone and teeth.

Minute remnants of brain or other tissues that have been scattered by gunshot or other trauma or tissue that might still adhere to the weapon or a bullet can sometimes yield sufficient DNA for testing. Bits of tissue such as these can be used if a body is not recovered and then identified by "reverse paternity," by comparison with surviving family members.

CHEMICALLY TREATED TISSUES

The two common chemical treatments are formaldehyde fixation for medical purposes and embalming. DNA can be successfully tested from both tissues. Bodies that have been buried for several years can even yield results. Most commonly, exhumations are required in paternity determinations, but they may also provide a known exemplar to compare with evidence in a forensic case.

HAIR ROOTS

One to five hair roots can contain sufficient tissue for RFLP analysis. Shed, or telogen, hairs contain only trace amounts of DNA, and are generally not suitable for testing by current methods in routine forensic use. A highly specialized method known as mitochondrial sequencing is beginning to be used more and more. It was this method that was recently used to identify one of Napoleon's hairs and members of the Romanoff family.

SALIVA

DNA can be typed from saliva deposited on envelope flaps or stamps, as was done in the New York World Trade Center bombings. It can also be taken from cigarette butts found at crime scenes, and even from cups, bottles, telephone mouthpieces, bite marks and penile swabs.

URINE

Success with DNA analysis of urine is less common, as healthy individuals do not shed nucleated cells into the urine. Conventional testing is more likely to yield results, and is used in disputes over samples that have been tested for drugs.

PRODUCTS OF CONCEPTION

The non-living products of conception most often analyzed are abortuses. Usually these cases stem from allegations of criminal paternity where a teenaged girl has been impregnated by a relative or other adult. Other cases might involve a prison guard accused of having sexual relations with an inmate or a rape resulting in pregnancy.

FROM CRIME SCENE TO LABORATORY

Once a crime has been discovered, the scene must be secured and access controlled. Anyone who traverses the scene may alter it and impair evidence that could contribute to a solution of the crime. It is usually during the first crucial minutes following a violent crime that evidence is lost. Medical personnel or persons who have discovered the crime in their efforts to help, may destroy or alter evidence. The first police officers on the scene may not be the most experienced. In a high profile or especially violent crime, police "brass" may feel compelled to observe the scene.

In addition to detectives, there may be personnel from a variety of agencies involved including death investigators from the medical examiner or coroner's office, evidence technicians from an identification unit, criminalists from the crime lab, and attorneys from the prosecutor's office. The relationships

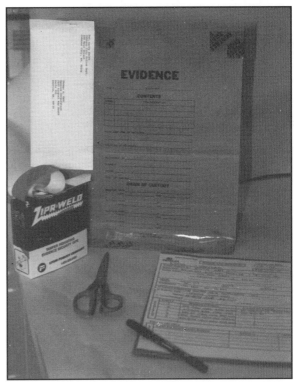

Sealed evidence bags, documented transfers, and rigorous record keeping maintain the chain of custody.

between these agencies may not always be models of cooperation. In the Simpson case, the defense has criticized the competence of the investigators. While the examples of substandard performance certainly are not laudable, many other American jurisdictions would not have done as well. Overworked, understaffed, inadequately funded crime labs are a reality in this country where the rhetoric of the war on crime is substantial and support of the infrastructure is not.

Criminalist examining an article of cloth- ing for semen stains.

In the case of rape, the victim's body is considered part of the crime scene and it is searched, combed, and probed. Any trace of the rapist —sperm, blood, hair, even saliva— is poten- tially incriminating. In order to maximize the amount and value of physical evidence obtained from a sexual assault victim, sam- ples should be collected as soon as possible. Showering, changing clothes, or otherwise cleaning up can severely compromise the abil- ity to collect usable evidence. If the victim is alive, this examina- tion is usually done in a hospital emergency room, sometimes by specially-trained physicians or nurses.

Once the scene is secured, searching for, identifying, photo- graphing, labeling, and gathering evidence are started. The chain of custody is established as the items of evidence enter the sys- tem. From this point on, it must be possible to document the exact whereabouts of the evidence at all times as it moves through the system, both within a particular agency and from agency to agency. Without the maintenance of the chain of cus- tody, the value of the evidence may be completely lost because it will be disal- lowed. Generally, the evidence is taken from a crime scene to a police evidence room until it is transferred to a crime laboratory. Most evidence is never analyzed unless and until a suspect is located.

Once in the crime lab, evidence is usually handled by a criminalist, a person trained in forensic sciences, ie. the study of the physical elements of a crime. A criminologist, on the other hand, is a social scientist who studies the behavior of the criminal, the social and psychological elements of crime, etc.

Prior to beginning DNA analysis, confirmatory testing is performed on questioned stains. These tests determine if the stain is blood, semen or saliva and if it is of human origin. Classical blood testing methods may be used to perform preliminary individualizing testing in an attempt to eliminate a suspect. These tests are much quicker and cheaper to perform than DNA tests. A combination of these common tests can eliminate the overwhelming majority of falsely-suspected individuals.

THE ADVANTAGES OF DNA EVIDENCE

The introduction of DNA typing to forensic science has brought about a revolution in the identification of body fluid stains and tissues. The use of classical blood typing of the ABO group as well as other less commonly known blood types, such as PGM, ESD, and others, allow forensic scientists to exclude an individual as the source of a blood stain but cannot unequivocally link a particular stain to a particular individual. These are the kinds of blood typing tests entered into evidence at the Simpson preliminary hearing and are a powerful tool for eliminating someone as an evidence source.

Environmental Effects on RFLP Tests	
Conditions	Can Be Tested

• Sunlight
  Moderate temp.
  Hot, humid weather
	up to 6 weeks
	10 days or less

• No Sunlight Hot weather	5 mos. or more

• Gas, oil, detergent,
  acid, base, salt, bleach,
  non-human DNA
	No effect

• Soil	Precludes test
adapted from FBI data	

The typical genetic profile that can be determined by conventional blood typing might be found in anywhere from 0.1% to 10% of the overall population. The genetic profiles obtained by DNA typing, in contrast, might be found in less than one in a few million or even billions of individuals. In other words, they can be unique or virtually unique in the human population.

```
Please Print or Type                                        Laboratory Case Number
GENELEX          ┌─────────────────────────────┐          ┌──────────────────────┐
                 │  FORENSIC ANALYSIS REQUEST  │          │  F 94 - 132          │
                 └─────────────────────────────┘          └──────────────────────┘
    ☒ New Case        ☐ Additional Evidence              ┌──────────────────────┐
                                                          │ DATE  11-15-94       │
Analysis Requested by:   DETECTIVE  HARRY  SMITH
Representing: JOHNSON CITY POLICE DEPT.  Phone: ( 206  )- 936 - 1722  Ext.
Mailing Address:         220  MAIN  STREET
                         JOHNSON CITY , WA.  98254


LEGAL        JOHNSON CITY            BLYTHE                 WA.
VENUE            city                county              state/province
COMMENTS:   TRIAL DATE    DEC. 16, 1994

EVIDENCE SUBMITTED  Date/Time: 11-15-94  10:22 AM  Accepted by: Aaw
☒ In person: Name    DETECTIVE  HARRY  SMITH
        Signature: St. Harry Smith  Badge #1104
☐ Carrier/Tracking # _____        ☐ US Mail # _____
```

	Exhibit #	Description of Evidence	Examination(s) Requested
S U B M I S S I O N	1	SHIRT r/ from SUSPECT JOSEPH DANNER	DNA EXTRACTION AND EVALUATION
	2	CIGARETTE BUTTS r/ from SCENE	DNA PROFILING
	3	RAPE KIT r/ from VICTIM KATHY DICKSON	
	4	BLOOD SAMPLE r/ from VICTIM KATHY DICKSON	
	5	BLOOD SAMPLE r/ from SUSPECT JOSEPH DANNER	

FOR LAB USE ONLY

	Exhibit Number(s)/Laboratory Employee	Released to:	DATE
R E L E A S E	1 TO 5 / TA.	Detective Harry Smith	12/2/94

Typical form for documenting the transfer of evidence items between individuals from two different agencies thereby maintaining the chain of custody.

Further limitations of conventional systems are that stains which are a mixture of fluids from two individuals can be difficult to interpret, because the proteins cannot be separated by simply separating the sperm from non-sperm cells, as is done in DNA testing. In fact, it is not possible to tell conclusively, with many non-DNA genetic tests, if a mixture of stains from more than one person is present. In addition, the classical genetic markers do not last nearly as long in samples that are exposed to the outdoor environment, and contamination by common chemicals or microorganisms have a rapidly destructive effect. DNA, in contrast, is extremely durable and comparatively resistant to contamination.

Moisture, sunlight, bacterial action and heat are detrimental to the DNA. Depending on the intensity and combination of these conditions, survival of the DNA is measured in weeks or months. Even so, DNA in usable amounts can often be recovered when no other test could be performed. DNA is particularly stable when dried. Once the sample is removed to a dry, cool, indoor environment, DNA survival in stains can be measured in years or even decades.

DNA in the Courtroom

Chapter 3

DNA in the Laboratory

BASIC GENETICS:
WHY DNA TYPING WORKS

There are about 100 trillion cells in the adult human body. Most of them have a nucleus, or center, that contains thread-like bundles of chromosomes. In these chromosomes are all of the instructions and information needed to make a human being. Each parent contributes one chromosome to each of the 23 pairs found in all normal people. Within the chromosomes, are up to 100,000 paired genes, the fundamental units of heredity. Each gene can have different versions (as many as 100 or more in rare cases) called alleles, but most are the same from person to person. Genes determine all inherited traits including those that give the individual specific characteristics (blue eyes rather than brown eyes) as well as common characteristics (two eyes, two arms, etc.).

Genes are made of deoxyribonucleic acid (DNA). Hence, DNA is the master molecule of life and controls the growth and development of every living thing. It is a

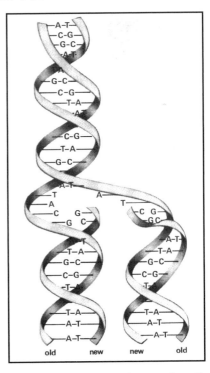

A diagram of a dividing and replicating DNA molecule showing the base pairings.

polymer, i.e., a long string of simple repeating units. These repeating units are called nucleotides and are of four types: adenine (A), cytosine (C), guanine (G), and thymine (T). Just as the order of the letters of the alphabet determines the information content of words, the order in which these four bases are strung together is what gives DNA its information content. The complete DNA molecule consists of two of these strands of the four bases.

In the two strands, A always is across from or paired with T and G always is paired with C. These are the base pairs that are the unit of measurement in determining the size of a given segment of DNA. This structure suggests a natural mechanism for the duplication or replication of the DNA molecule, as occurs during cell division. These pairings are what connect the two strands of DNA together to form a tightly coiled, twisted ladder. This spiral staircase, the famous double helix, is the natural form in which DNA is found within the nucleus of the cells.

If uncoiled, the DNA molecules in every human cell would measure six feet in length. That is the total length of the 3.3 billion base pairs that make up the total human genetic complement or genome. Except for identical twins, the sequence of the base pairs within the DNA helix is unique for every person, and forms the individual's genetic code or blueprint.

Perhaps the basis of DNA typing can be best understood by comparing the way in which genetic information is stored in the DNA to the way in which printed information is stored in books. For example, if we were to cut all the sentences in forty volumes of the Encyclopedia Britannica into strips, and tape them together end to end, then we would have an amount of information equivalent to that contained in the DNA within each of the cells that make up our bodies. Furthermore, the information would then be in the same physical form as the DNA information, i.e., a long linear strip sometimes likened to a computer punch tape.

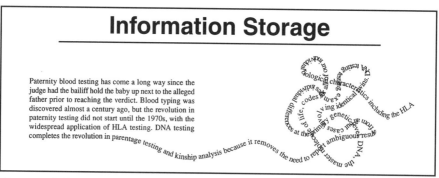

Information Storage

Paternity blood testing has come a long way since the judge had the bailiff hold the baby up next to the alleged father prior to reaching the verdict. Blood typing was discovered almost a century ago, but the revolution in paternity testing did not start until the 1970s, with the widespread application of HLA testing. DNA testing completes the revolution in parentage testing and kinship analysis because it removes the need to rely on the master...

The way information is stored genetically can be compared to the way it is stored within a written text.

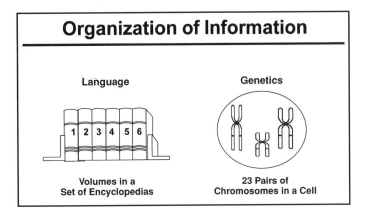

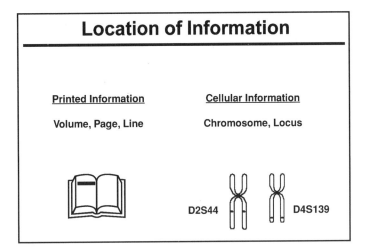

The genetic information contained in the DNA is organized and packaged into chromosomes, much as printed information is organized into volumes. Just as a specific passage in the encyclopedia can be identified by specifying a volume, page, and line number, a specific genetic passage or location, known as a locus, can be identified. A specific naming system identifies genes by numbers issued by the Human Gene Mapping Committee. For example, if we see the designation D4S139 in a report, then we know exactly what gene has been analyzed, that it is on chromosome four, and that it is the 139th DNA probe to be mapped to chromosome four.

A significant difference between the way information is stored in the cell and in the encyclopedia is that there are two copies of the information in each of the cells, one from the mother and one from the father. These two copies of the genetic information which are largely identical, come together at the moment of conception when the sperm and the egg join together. All of the child's cells contain DNA derived from this original fertilized cell, half from the mother and half from the father. It is this basic principle of heredity, first discovered over 150 years ago, that allows us to reliably perform parentage tests.

What is DNA?

1. DNA is the chemical substance which makes up our chromosomes and controls all inheritable traits (*i.e.* eye, hair, and skin color)
2. DNA is different for every individual except identical twins
3. DNA is found in all cells with a nucleus (white blood cells, soft tissue cells, bone cells, hair root cells, and spermatozoa)
4. Half of an individual's DNA/chromosomes come from the father, the other half from the mother
5. DNA is a double-stranded molecule
6. The DNA strands are made of four different building blocks: A connects with T, G connects with C
7. The four building blocks and their sequence in DNA makes up the letters of the genetic code
8. An individual's DNA remains the same throughout life
9. In specific regions on a DNA strand each person has a unique sequence of building blocks or genetic code
10. It is a person's unique genetic code that allows scientists to identify an individual to the exclusion of all others

Size of Various Genetic Elements

Cells in the body	100 trillion
Chromosomes in each cell	23 pairs
DNA in each cell	6 ft. long
DNA in each cell	3.3 billion base pairs
Typical gene	20-100 thousand base pairs
Typical VNTR	1-20 thousand base pairs
Typical VNTR repeat unit	15-75 base pairs
Restriction enzyme site	4-6 base pairs

VARIABLE DNA:
THE KEY TO DNA TYPING

The DNA and hence the genetic code of humans is almost the same for all individuals. It is the very small amount that differs from person to person that forensic scientists analyze to identify people. These differences are called polymorphisms (from the Greek for "many forms") and are the key to DNA typing.

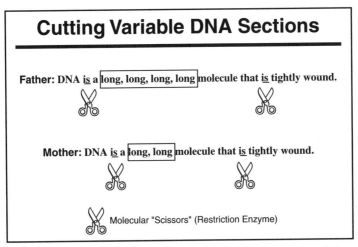

Cutting Variable DNA Sections

Father: DNA is a long, long, long, long molecule that is tightly wound.

Mother: DNA is a long, long molecule that is tightly wound.

Molecular "Scissors" (Restriction Enzyme)

A continuation of the analogy between DNA and the printed word showing how the length of DNA varies from person to person.

Variation in the DQA Gene

1.1 Ther**R** are six versions of the DQA gene

1.2 The**E**e are six versions of the DQA gene

1.3 T**T**ere are six versions of the DQA gene

2.0 There are six **B**ersions of the DQA gene

3.0 There are six versions of the DQA **J**ene

4.0 There are si**S** versions of the DQA gene

The bolded, enlarged letters show how the change of a single letter (base pair) is the basis for variation in the DQA1 gene.

Two major kinds of polymorphisms are most useful to forensic scientists. The first consists of variations in the length of the DNA at specific locations (loci) known as VNTRs (variable number of tandem repeats). These VNTR regions consist of stretches of DNA made up of short repeating DNA sequences. The number of times the short DNA sequence is repeated determines the physical length of the DNA molecule at these specific loci. Each of the many versions that may be found in the population are known as alleles. These variations are examined by the method known as the RFLP technique. The second type of variation in the DNA is simply a difference in the nucleotide letters found at a specific pair of bases. These are examined by the method known as PCR.

The goals are the same for both types of DNA tests: to isolate a distinctive DNA sequence and record its presence in a way that can be examined visually. The basic procedure of RFLP analysis is known as "Southern blotting" after Edward Southern, a Scottish bio-chemist who developed the technique in the early 1970s. The basic procedures of PCR based testing were invented in the early 1980s by Kary Mullis while working for a California biotechnology company.

Deciding which method to use is determined by the amount of DNA that is available and how deteriorated or degraded it is. RFLP analysis is more often performed because it is more discriminating. If there is only a small amount of material or it is highly degraded, PCR analysis is used, because this method requires less material and can produce a result on DNA of poor quality. As little as two billionths of a gram (2 ng), the amount of DNA contained in about 700 sperm cells will suffice for PCR analysis. The RFLP test requires 20 to 50 ng of DNA. PCR tests can be performed in a matter of days as compared to weeks for RFLP tests.

Comparison of Forensic DNA Analysis Methods

	RFLP	PCR
Discrimination Ability	"DNA Fingerprinting"	DQA ~ 1/8-1/50 Polymarker ~ 1/1000
Application	Most cases	Insufficient DNA for RFLP analysis
Sensitivity	>50 nanograms	>2 nanograms
Turnaround	4-8 weeks	2-3 days
Cost	$1200-$1500	$1200-$1500

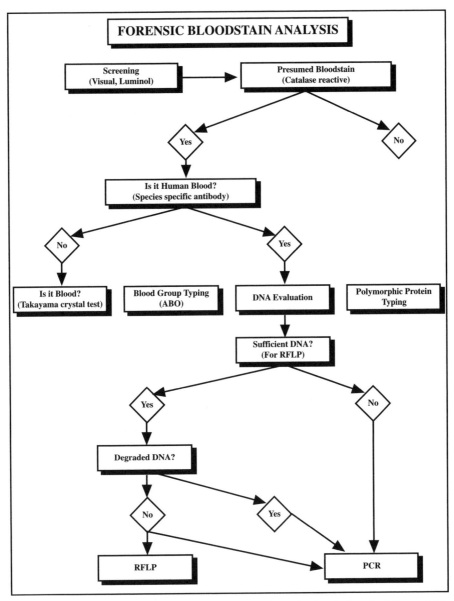

Screening of specimens by a variety of methods is the basis for deciding which DNA test to use.

DNA EVALUATION

Once the evidence has been documented and screened in the laboratory, and deemed appropriate for DNA analysis, the initial step is to isolate or purify the DNA. First, it must be removed from whatever object it is attached to and removed from the cell. Unless the major non-DNA constituents of the cell such as proteins, fats and carbohydrates are removed, the enzymes essential in the next step will not be able to do their work. This isolation of DNA begins with the controlled destruction of cellular integrity, releasing the DNA from its nuclear and chromosomal packaging. The cell walls are dissolved with a detergent and the proteins are digested by enzymes.

The DNA then is purified by the methods of extraction and precipitation. Once the DNA is isolated and concentrated, a small sample is tested to determine quality and quantity. If intact (high molecular weight) human DNA is present in sufficient amounts, RFLP testing can proceed. If the DNA is degraded, or present in minute amounts, PCR testing is used.

RESTRICTION FRAGMENT LENGTH POLYMORPHISM (RFLP) ANALYSIS

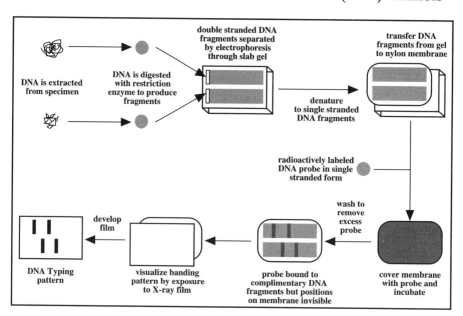

RFLP typing of purified DNA consists of the following six steps:
1. Cutting the DNA into pieces (Restriction Enzyme Digestion);
2. Separating the DNA by size (Gel Electrophoresis);

3. Transferring the DNA to a solid support surface (Southern Transfer);
4. Targeting and visualizing the DNA of interest (Hybridization and Autoradiography);
5. Reading the DNA profile (Interpretation of Data); and
6. Determining the rarity of the DNA profile (Population Genetics and Frequency Estimates).

RESTRICTION ENZYME DIGESTION

Restriction enzymes reproducibly cut DNA at specific four or six-base-pair sequences called restriction sites. *Hae* III *(Haemophilus Aegyptius III)*, the most commonly used enzyme in forensic science, cuts the DNA everywhere the bases are arranged in the sequence GGCC. These sites are found throughout the human genome and are, for the most part, the same in everyone. *Hae* III cuts human DNA into approximately 12 million different restriction fragments ranging in size from a few hundred to 10,000 or more base pairs in length.

GEL ELECTROPHORESIS

The physical length of DNA restriction fragments in VNTRs is one fundamental biochemical characteristic that varies from person to person. Electrophoresis is the technique by which the different-sized fragments are separated. The DNA is loaded into a hole, or well, at one end of a slab of semi-solid

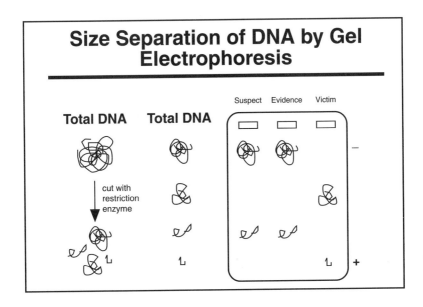

Size Separation of DNA by Gel Electrophoresis

gel, a porous, Jello-like substance. When an electrical field is applied to the gel containing the DNA, the DNA moves toward the positive electrode because it has a negative electrical charge.

The sieving action of the gel allows the small restriction fragments to migrate at a faster rate than the larger ones, just as a small rabbit would move faster and farther through a thicket than a large hound in pursuit. The relative position of these fragments within the gel after overnight current application is determined by their length or molecular weight.

Gels have several lanes within them which contain DNA, including marker lanes that measure how far fragments move through the gel and a lane for control DNA that produces a known pattern and can be used to verify that the test was properly conducted. The DNA in the gel can be stained and seen under ultraviolet (black) light.

Forensic lab analysts loading DNA evidence samples into electrophoresis gels.

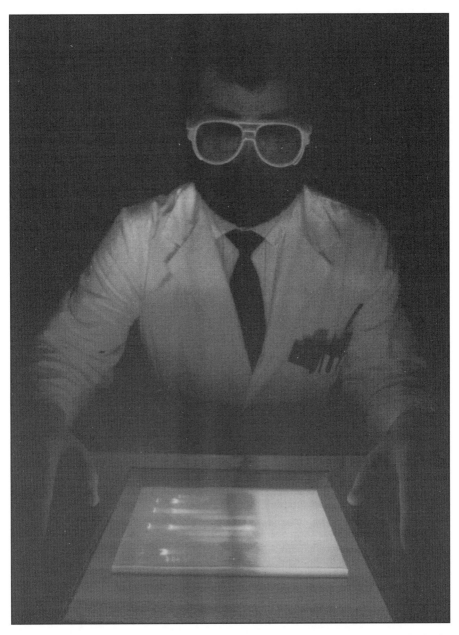

A gel stained with a DNA specific dye illuminated by ultraviolet (black) light.

SOUTHERN TRANSFER

Because the gel is fragile, it is necessary to remove the DNA from the gel and permanently attach it to a solid support. This is accomplished by the process of Southern blotting. The first step is to denature the DNA in the gel which means that the double-stranded restriction fragments are chemically separated into the single-stranded form. The DNA then is transferred by the process of blotting to a sheet of nylon. The nylon acts like an ink blotter and "blots" up the separated DNA fragments. The restriction fragments, invisible at this stage, are irreversibly attached to the positively-charged nylon membrane called the "blot."

DNA PROBES

Visual observation of an individual's DNA pattern requires the use of DNA probes. The DNA probe, like a guided missile, will seek out and find its target sequence. There are approximately a dozen VNTR DNA probes in common usage in forensic RFLP testing. These probes have been patented and are commercially available from biotechnology suppliers. Each DNA probe can be used to develop the DNA profile at a particular VNTR locus. Most of these are located on different chromosomes, an important factor to be considered when performing a statistical analysis. Most forensic tests use a combination of at least four to six separate DNA probes in a sequential manner. All of these DNA probes have been obtained by the process of cloning, which simply means that they are free of all other human DNA. Therefore, large quantities of probe DNA can be made and labeled with a radioactive or other tracer in the laboratory.

HYBRIDIZATION

To detect a VNTR locus immobilized on the Southern blot, one uses a DNA probe that has a base pair sequence complimentary to the DNA sequence at the VNTR locus. The double-stranded nature of DNA and a phenomenon called hybridization provide the scientific basis for the usefulness of DNA probes. Double-stranded DNA fragments will separate when heated. When the DNA cools down, the two strands will reconnect and become double-stranded again. This is not a random process. Because of the complementarity of the two DNA strands, the single strands will only reconnect with another strand that has a complimentary sequence.

Just prior to its use, the DNA probe is labeled with a radioactive or other tracer and boiled to the single stranded form. The DNA on the blot, also single stranded, is soaked or incubated in a solution containing the DNA probe. The probe hybridizes, or binds, to only the DNA fragments that bear the complimentary sequences of DNA bases. These will be the restriction fragments corresponding to the locus from which the probe was originally cloned.

AUTORADIOGRAPHY

The excess probe is washed off and the blot placed in contact with a sheet of film. The film, exposed by the radioactive tracer instead of light, is developed and becomes an autoradiograph, commonly known as an autorad. The autorad is the final product of the RFLP analysis. It reveals the overall quality of the testing and can be copied, distributed and interpreted by other DNA experts.

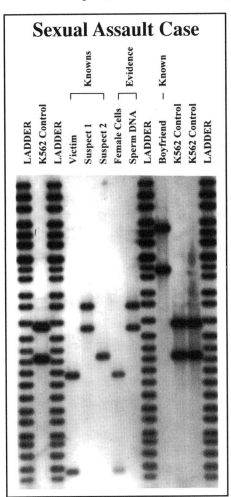

Sexual Assault Case

The autorad has darkened areas known as bands corresponding to the position of the DNA probes and hence the restriction fragments bound to the membrane. Typically, several probes are used sequentially in order to compile forensically significant DNA profiles. This requires that the blot be stripped of the first radioactive probe, hybridized to a second, washed and exposed to a new film to make another autorad. Each round of hybridization and autoradiography may take up to ten days. This is why RFLP testing takes longer than conventional blood or PCR testing.

A typical layout of samples on a sexual assault case autorad. The sperm DNA found on a vaginal swab taken from a rape victim matches suspect one's DNA. The victim's blood DNA also matches the non-sperm DNA found on the swab. Suspect two and the boyfriend are excluded.

INTERPRETATION OF DATA

Up to this point in DNA analysis, there is little argument about its validity (provided that it is done correctly) because we are dealing with physical reality. The interpretation of the data, what is its meaning, is another story. This requires that inferences based on the science of statistics, population genetics and probability theory be applied to the measurements of physical reality that the autorads reveal.

Forensic scientists use these mathematical concepts to calculate and report an estimate of how frequently the genetic profile they have observed might be found in major population groups. If the genetic profiles found in two different samples, say one from a piece of evidence and one from a suspect are indistinguishable, they are said to match. A typical population frequency for conventional blood typing might be 1 in 200, for DNA 1 in 5,000,000. This means that only 1 in 5,000,000 people would have the same DNA profile. All others would be excluded from being the source of the matching evidence.

Irrespective of what calculation method is used, it is a physical fact that the genetic profiles match and that they would be found at some frequency in the population. In attempting to call the frequency estimates into question, attorneys are fond of pointing out that they are a comparison between the observed profile and randomly chosen individuals, and that a relative of the person with the profile is much more likely to share that profile than any of the random individuals.

When forensic scientists provide a report and testimony about the frequency estimates, their job is done. The judgment of guilt or innocence reached by the court may take these estimates into account, but they must be placed into the circumstances surrounding the crime and the intent, motive, means and opportunity available to the defendant.

COMMON FALLACIES

The meaning of the genetic profile frequencies are often misconstrued by attorneys. For example, the argument might be made that if a pair of matching genetic profiles are found in 1 in 200 individuals then there is a 1 in 200 chance that they came from different sources. Not true. What the chance is that they came from different sources cannot be determined by the genetic evidence alone. It depends on all of the circumstances surrounding the case.

Another fallacy is the one heard in the Simpson case preliminary hearing. O.J. Simpson's blood type matched blood found on the sidewalk trailing away from the murder scene. Defense attorneys pointed out that 80,000 people in Los Angeles share that blood type. True, but all of those 80,000 people didn't visit 85 South Bundy where the homicides occurred.

The prosecutor's fallacy is to argue that as the genetic profile is found in 1 in 1000 people then there is only a 1 in 1000 chance that the defendant is innocent. Once again this ignores the other facts of the case and asks the scientific evidence to determine guilt or innocence. Science cannot do that. Guilt or innocence must be determined by the judge or jury.

EVALUATING THE ARGUMENTS

Critics of DNA testing have generated and seized upon disagreements about the best way to interpret the data as a reason not to admit DNA evidence. Forensic scientists themselves have given the critics ammunition by not always following widely used scientific conventions for rounding off and reporting the significance of the numbers that are reported.

In evaluating the criticisms that are made, primarily of the validity of the population data on which probability estimates are made, it is important to remember that the critics:

- If they are geneticists at all, study non-human organisms or came to the study of human genetics from other fields. None are forensic scientists.
- Use the same assumptions in their own work that they argue against in forensic science.
- Base their critiques on overdrawn hypothetical and theoretical arguments for which no data exists.
- Ignore the safeguards and quality programs that are routinely used by forensic DNA labs.

Much of the population genetics controversy has been generated by an elementary misunderstanding of the basics of RFLP testing in the early writing of Eric Lander. Another source of misunderstanding was an article published in 1972 by Richard Lewontin and since repudiated by the author. Long after Lewontin changed his mind, the article continued to be used to support defense motions to quash DNA evidence.

What this reveals is that one defense strategy is the shotgun approach; throw up a barrage of flak and hope that the judge or jury accepts the validity of at least one of the arguments. The critics also change their arguments over time. As various lines of attack are countered or exposed as spurious, new objections are raised. Frequency estimates are fertile territory for the attackers because most people are not conversant with the methods of statistics and the meaning of probability.

The first step in the analysis of an autorad is visual inspection.

READING THE AUTORAD

Before an opinion can be formed as to the forensic significance of a set of DNA profiles, a series of data interpretation steps must be completed.

- First, the examiner inspects the case specific data and records to determine if procedures have been followed and interpretable results have been produced.
- Second, a visual inspection of the autorad is made and an opinion of the testing results is formed. Is the suspect included or excluded from the group of individuals who could be the source of the evidence?
- Third, computerized electronic measurements and statistical calculations are made that must confirm the examiner's visual "match" calls.
- Finally, probability calculations using population genetic data are used to calculate a conservative estimate of the occurrence of the DNA profile in major population groups.

In forensic science, statistics are used to ensure that the data is interpreted in a conservative fashion, that it can be guaranteed to be an overstatement of the true occurrence of a DNA profile in the population. For example, if we were to test everybody in the entire world then we would know exactly how often a given genetic profile occurs. Let's say that it is 1 in a million. If we report that profile out at 1 in 500,000, that is acceptable because it is an understatement. The data has been systematically skewed in favor of the defendant.

VISUAL INTERPRETATION

The purpose of the visual inspection is to form an opinion as to which of the DNA samples in the various lanes in the autorad could have come from the same individual source and which could not. Included in the autorad are bands from any DNA that was tested as well as control specimens from known individuals. In order to be valid, the opinion formed at this stage must be confirmed by the following quantitative tests.

DNA FRAGMENT SIZE ESTIMATION

Central to the analysis are the series of "sizing ladders" containing up to 30 closely spaced bands. Each of the bands in the sizing ladders corresponds to a fragment of DNA of exactly known size. These are the rulers which computerized video devices use to measure the DNA fragments in each of the sample lanes. The estimated size of the fragments being measured are reported in base pairs.

At least one sample of a human DNA, known as K562, is run on virtually every membrane used in forensic casework. The K562 DNA is available as a standard reference material from the National Institute of Standards and Technology. Sizing estimates of the K562 must be within established tolerances before sizing estimates from that membrane are acceptable.

This video scanning device, developed by the FBI, is used to estimate the size of DNA bands seen on an autorad. Data from this device will be used to confirm the examiners match calls.

BAND COMPARISONS BY "MATCH CRITERIA"

Comparisons are made between the DNA profiles of the known samples (generally blood samples taken from the suspect and/or victim) and DNA profiles of the evidence samples (for example, bloodstains from the crime scene or dried vaginal swabs). There are three possible results:

1. There is a match between two specimens being compared. If the match is between a suspect and the DNA in the evidence, then that suspect is included in the group of individuals who could be the source of that evidence;

2. There is not a match between the samples. The suspect could not be the source of the evidence. They are excluded from the group of individuals who could have contributed the specimen; or

3. The data is inconclusive, meaning that it is not possible to make a determination. This can be caused by a variety of factors, and usually occurs when the DNA is old and heavily contaminated.

Interpretation of RFLP data has required the adoption of statistical techniques new to forensic serology because of the numeric nature of the data. In ABO and other typing systems, the data is a non-numeric listing of discrete types. In the RFLP technique, the sizing estimates form a continuous distribution because restriction fragments differing by one VNTR repeat unit cannot be distinguished. Therefore, it becomes necessary to perform statistical calculations to determine if two bands on an autorad can be distinguished from one another.

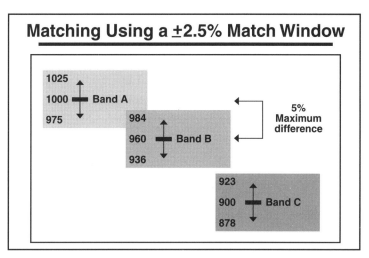

Matching Using a ±2.5% Match Window

Bands A and B match, band C does not.

For forensic purposes, two DNA profiles are said to match if they are statistically indistinguishable and are therefore consistent with having been produced by DNA from the same individual. First a quantitative match range for each appropriate VNTR band is calculated. Next the match ranges of corresponding bands are compared lane to lane. If these ranges overlap then the bands are indistinguishable from one another and are said to match. The process continues until all bands at a locus, and all bands at all the loci examined have been compared. In order for two composite DNA profiles to be declared a match and therefore included in the group of DNA profiles that could have come from an individual source, all bands must match.

Most laboratories use a match range, or "window", on the order of + 2.5% of the measured size or molecular weight of the band. This match window has been determined by comparing the DNA profiles obtained from vaginal swabs and fresh blood from rape victims. When working with fresh blood samples, such as in a parentage laboratory, the measurement error is less than 1% of the measured size of the bands.

BANDSHIFTING

The relatively large size of the forensic match window compensates for the phenomenon known as "bandshifting". When DNA fragments are separated by electrophoresis, each sample is loaded into its own lane on the gel. Sometimes, in poor quality samples, the DNA in one lane can travel faster or slower than those in other lanes. This phenomenon is known as band shifting and complicates the direct comparison of samples. If it is severe, it can lead to a false negative result, an exclusion that clears the suspect even though he is actually the source of the specimen.

POPULATION GENETICS AND FREQUENCY ESTIMATES.

There are only two reasons a pair of DNA profiles would match:
- The profiles came from the same individual. If the profiles do come from the same individual, then that is a certainty and no statistical probability is necessary; or
- The profiles came from two different and unrelated individuals, who share a genetic pattern. To address this possibility, a conservative statistical estimate as to how frequently the DNA profile in question might occur in the general population is formulated.

If two DNA profiles are found to match, then it is important to explain the significance of that match. Drawing these conclusions relies on population data bases that are surveys of DNA profiles from populations of unrelated individuals.

BINNING

The data from the populations is analyzed by the process of binning which converts it into tables that can be referred to in order to determine what percentage of the population has a particular observed band. The use of binning and the way in which these tables are prepared is the most important safeguard for ensuring that the data is interpreted in a manner favorable to the suspect.

The size of the bins determines how conservative will be the interpretation of the data. For example, if we had a very accurate device for measuring foot size and we measured the feet of a hundred individuals they almost all would be different. Those one hundred people would all fit into three sizes of beach shoes, five or six sizes of whole-number-sized shoes, and a dozen half-sized shoes. Assigning the foot sizes that we measured to one of these sets of sizes would be similar to the process of binning.

If we were to observe a footprint at a crime scene and wanted to determine how often that size print occurred in the population, we would go to the table of binned shoe sizes that we had previously collected. By looking up the frequency of occurrence of the bin into which the foot size that we found fits, we would be able to provide a conservative estimate of how often it would be found in the general population. Obviously, which table we use determines how conservative is our interpretation of the data. The binning system that is commonly used in forensic laboratories underestimates the true rarity of most DNA profiles by a factor of five or ten.

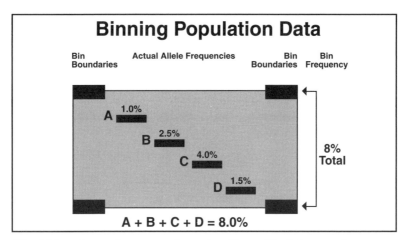

Fixed bins chosen for convenience to align with sizing markers actually contain several alleles of low frequency. The higher frequency of the bin is used for all bands that fall into that bin.

HARDY-WEINBERG PRINCIPLE

In practice, the size estimates for each band are assigned to a bin and the frequency values for each of the bins are multiplied together. The basis for this process is known as the Hardy-Weinberg principle. This principle was independently discovered by both Hardy and Weinberg in the early part of the century. It states that the presence of a particular allele of a gene at a locus has no predictive value as to what the other allele will be. This is the result of random mating in the population. In other words, the two events are independent.

LINKAGE EQUILIBRIUM AND THE PRODUCT RULE

After the individual frequencies for each VNTR gene pair are calculated, they all can be multiplied together because the genes that are used are said to be in linkage equilibrium. That means that they would tend not to be inherited together. What happens at one VNTR locus is independent of what happens at other unlinked loci. These computations are made according to the "product rule."

Multiplication of the frequencies assigned to the individual bands typically results in the estimation of frequencies of extraordinary rarity. Obviously, the more DNA systems examined, the more rare the DNA profile.

	Calculating a DNA Profile Frequency		
Locus	**Band Bin Frequencies**	**Locus Frequency**	**Combined Frequency**
	Band 1/Band 2		
1	0.08/0.02 (8%) (2%)	0.003 or 1 in 333	----
2	0.15/0.04	0.012 or 1 in 83	1 in 28 thousand
3	0.08/0.06	0.010 or 1 in 100	1 in 3 million
4	0.22/0.09	0.040 or 1 in 25	1 in 70 million

The most common RFLP test uses four VNTR loci.

POPULATION DATABASES

Population data is collected, banked and reported separately for the three major racial/ethnic groups of Blacks, Caucasians, and Hispanics. There also are data bases available for a variety of Asian, Native American and other groups. These have been compiled in what has come to be called "The Worldwide Study," a five-volume set of population data compiled and published by the F.B.I. The genetic profile frequency of the evidence is usually reported out for each of the three major groups or for any others that may be relevant to the case or that are requested to be calculated and reported. It might seem that the logical database to use would be the one in which the defendant is included racially or ethnically, but in fact we have no way to know the race of the individual who donated the evidence sample. Race or ethnicity cannot be determined by DNA.

While there are statistically significant differences between these data bases, the differences are small and, within the context of a multi-chromosome DNA profile, of negligible practical and forensic significance. The use of these databases is not appropriate if there is a close relative of the accused who also could have donated the evidence.

THE CEILING PRINCIPLE

The ceiling principle is the highly controversial method suggested by the NRC report, *DNA Technology in Forensic Science*, for calculating DNA profile frequencies. For the purposes of reaching a consensus solution on reporting frequencies the NRC assumed "that population substructure might exist" to such an extent that it could cause the calculations to be biased against the defendant. The ceiling principle factors this possibility in by establishing the highest frequency for each DNA site in three major population groups—Caucasian, Hispanic, and Afro-American. By using this number or 10%, whichever was higher, probability estimates would favor the suspect even more than those derived from the match binning methods then in use. The use of 10% is the interim ceiling principle. When a prescribed set of studies is completed this can be dropped to the ceiling principle which would lower the "ceiling" from 10% to 5%.

GENELEX   IDENTITY TEST RESULTS

GeneLex Corporation
2203 Airport Way South, Suite 350, Seattle, Washington 98134
Telephone: 206.382.9591 Fax: 206.382.6277

October 5, 1993

We have completed an identity analysis on samples from the individuals listed below. Based on the scientific evidence, we conclude that Q1-Bloodstain on Wood Trim and Q3-Bloodstain on Tile came from the same source, believed to be from victim, ▬▬▬▬▬.

Specimens analyzed:
    Q1-Bloodstain on Wood Trim
    Q3-Bloodstain on Tile

GeneLex Laboratory # F93-026 A (Homicide: ▬▬▬▬▬ - Victim)

System	Estimated fragment length (kb) Q1	Q3	Estimated Profile frequency Black/Caucasian/SW Hispanic
DNA Locus (Probe)/HaeIII			
D2S44(pYNH24)/Hae III	3.27/1.79	3.21/1.75	0.007/0.019/0.014
D4S139(pH30)/Hae III	9.17/8.66	9.16/8.55	0.017/0.025/0.046
D10S28(pTBQ7)/Hae III	2.69/1.39	2.65/1.37	0.005/0.003/0.004
D17S79(pV1)/Hae III	1.73/1.50	1.70/1.48	0.042/0.105/0.044
D14S13(pCMM101)/Hae III	4.27/1.98	4.21/1.95	0.006/0.002/0.004

Cumulative Profile frequency =	1 in 6.7 billion for Black
	1 in 3.3 billion for Caucasian
	1 in 2.2 billion for SW Hispanic

A match was found at every allele examined between Q1-Bloodstain on Wood Trim DNA profile and that of Q3-Bloodstain on Tile. The occurrence of the DNA profile exhibited by Q1-Bloodstain on Wood Trim is approximately 1 in 6.7 billion for African-Americans; approximately 1 in 3.3 billion for Caucasian Americans; and approximately 1 in 2.2 billion for Southwest Hispanic Americans.

Testing was performed according to the criteria outlined in the American Association of Blood Banks Parentage Testing Standards and the FBI's Technical Working Group on DNA Analysis Methods (TWGDAM).

Howard C. Coleman, BS   Laura J. Mendoza-Sandor, MS MT(ASCP)   Teresa H. Aulinskas, PhD
President   Laboratory Manager   Laboratory Director

State of Washington
County of King

On this _8th_ day of _October_, 19_93_, the named individual(s) personally appeared before me a notary public, and they being known to me as employees of GeneLex Corporation, did execute the foregoing and they did so as their free act and deed and that the same is true to the best of their knowledge and belief.

Notary Public _Joyce A Blair_   My commission expires _8-24-97_

JOYCE A. BLAIR
STATE OF WASHINGTON
NOTARY --•-- PUBLIC
My Commission Expires 8-24-97

A typical report comparing the DNA profiles found on two pieces of evidence that follows the convention of reporting the profile frequencies for three major population groups.

POLYMERASE CHAIN REACTION
(PCR) ANALYSIS

The polymerase chain reaction, or PCR as it is known, is used to analyze very small or poor quality DNA samples in forensic casework. PCR was invented in 1984 by Kary Mullis. The technique has such wide utility and is so simple to understand and use that it has been adopted at a pace unparalleled in the history of biological science. It is such a powerful technique for studying DNA that Mullis was awarded the Nobel prize in 1994 for its invention, an unusual event because the Nobel prize is normally awarded for a lifetime of work or for a broader discovery than a single experimental technique.

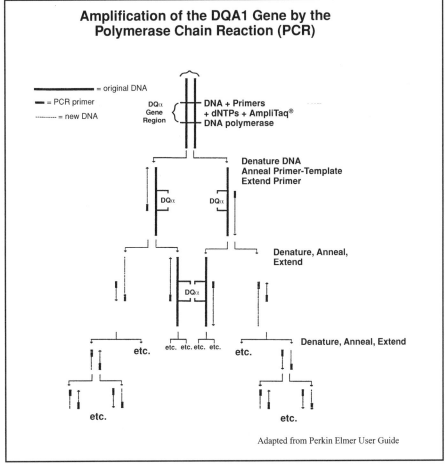

Amplification of the DQA1 Gene by the Polymerase Chain Reaction (PCR)

Adapted from Perkin Elmer User Guide

The amount of DNA doubles with each PCR cycle so that the amount of DNA produced increases geometrically.

What makes the PCR technique so valuable is that it gives scientists a method of copying very small sections of DNA. For example, in the most common forensic PCR test, the HLA DQA1 test, tens of millions of copies of a 240 base pair stretch of the DQA1 gene are made in the laboratory. The result is that the gene can be rapidly typed on the basis of very small samples. In theory, as little as one cell is sufficient to perform a PCR analysis. In practice the minimum number of cells that can be tested is about three or four hundred. PCR analysis has been referred to as "molecular xeroxing."

PCR analysis of DQA1 uses small DNA probes known as primers and the phenomenon of hybridization in a different way than they are used to detect a gene in the Southern blotting method previously described. In this instance they are used to define and start the PCR process by interacting not only with the DNA that will be tested, but also with a DNA polymerize a DNA replicating enzyme.

Taq DNA POLYMERASE

Taq DNA Polymerase is an enzyme isolated from *Thermus aquaticus*, a bacteria found in Yellowstone Park's geysers and hot springs. This enzyme has thoroughly adapted to its environment and can survive extended incubation at 95°C, just below the boiling point of water, the temperature required to denature or unzip the DNA strands. Virtually no other ordinary enzyme stays active at this temperature. So remarkable is *Taq* that it was chosen by *Science* magazine as the "Molecule of the Year" in 1989.

The DNA strands that are to be tested are referred to as the template, and the DNA probes are called the primers. In order to start the process, the template or test DNA is mixed with the primers and the four DNA building blocks A, G, T and C along with the *Taq* DNA Polymerase. The template DNA is separated into single strands by heating. As the solution of template DNA and primers cools down, the primers bind to both strands of the DQA1 gene. At this point, the *Taq* DNA Polymerase recognizes the combination of the template and primer as a place to start making new DNA.

New DNA is made, separated by heating and then cooled again so that more of the primers can bind to the original template DNA and to the newly made strands as well. The enzyme does its work again and the process is repeated. The amount of DQA1 gene DNA that is made increases geometrically. There are two strands after the first cycle, four after the second, eight after the third and so on. In an actual test of the DQA1 gene, the cycle will be repeated 30 times and millions of copies of the original DNA will be produced.

HLA DQA1 TYPING

The different versions of the HLA DQA1 gene are detected by the reverse dot blot method. Extracted DNA is added to a PCR reaction mix and placed into a thermal cycler to amplify the DQA1. The amplified DNA is incubated with typing strips containing immobilized DNA probes specific to the different DQA1 alleles. Following hybridization, a color development procedure is used to detect the presence of specific DQA1 alleles in the sample. The DQA1 type of a sample is determined by reading the pattern of blue dots.

This dot blot method depends once again on the phenomenon of DNA hybridization. The PCR product DNA binds only to the dots that correspond to its type based on the complimentary base pairs. If there is even one base difference, the DNA will not bind to that probe.

There are only six versions of the DQA1 gene, which explains why it is not nearly as valuable for identifying stains. Because each person has two versions of the gene there are twenty-one possible combinations of pairs of the gene,

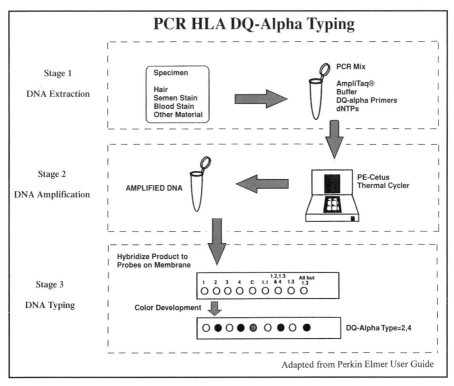

The reverse dot blot method used to detect the DQA1 gene can be completed in a day.

including those who have two copies of the same allele. They are known as homozygotes at the DQA1 locus and the people with two different alleles are known as heterozygotes. Each of the twenty-one different genotypes detected by the DQA1 system are found in from two to twelve percent of the general population.

The statistical and population genetic analysis of PCR-produced data is much simpler than that produced in RFLP because there isn't the problem of dealing with a continuous distribution of data. Similar to the methods used in conventional blood typing, one simply looks up the occurrence of the particular PCR- generated genotype in the population or populations of interest. This is true for almost all of the DNA analysis methods that are based on the PCR reaction.

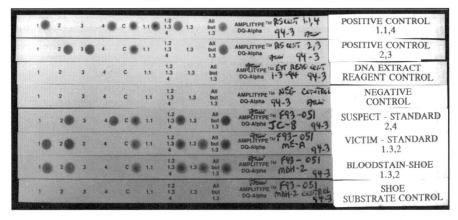

The pattern of the darker dots on the test strips are used to read the DQA1 genotype. The DQA1 type on the suspects shoe (1.3, 2) matches the victims, but not his own (2, 4)

POLYMARKER TYPING AND MULTIPLEXING

Polymarker typing works like DQA1 typing except that it tests five genes at once. These five genes each have their own set of primers and are amplified and detected simultaneously by the same method that is used for the DQA1 gene. This method of amplifying more than one gene at once is called multiplexing. Polymarker typing is conducted using the reverse dot blot format with the resultant pattern of blue dots indicating the genotype of the tested samples.

Because the genes that are used in the polymarker test have only two or three alleles, the information content of each gene is low. But taken together and combined with DQA1, they can detect DNA profiles that occur in from about one in a thousand to one in four thousand individuals.

AMPFLPS AND STRS

These are names for the latest testing methods that combine the advantages of both PCR and RFLP testing. In these tests the PCR method is used to amplify VNTR loci that are very small. This evolved into the names "short tandem repeats" (STRs) and "amplified fragment length polymorphisms" (AMPFLPs). The tandem repeats that are used in RFLP testing are not suitable because they are too large for successful amplification by PCR. After the STR is amplified, they are separated by size on a gel and visualized by staining or other methods, some of which are automated.

The most validated of these loci is D1S80 which was developed in large part by the FBI and is coming into widespread use. In fact, it may turn up in the Simpson trial. The D1S80 locus is a VNTR in which a 16 base pair sequence is repeated multiple times. Additional STR loci are being validated rapidly and brought on line. It is anticipated that in a few years, STRs will completely replace most other forms of DNA testing and become the standard technology in the foreseeable future.

STRs have a substantial advantage over the RFLP test in that alleles that differ by only one repeat unit can be separated on the gel and clearly distinguished from one another. Therefore methods such as binning are not required and the statistical calculations are not as difficult to understand and perform. The arguments over statistical interpretations that have complicated the acceptance of RFLP typing will be considerably fewer. Ironically, because these are discrete allele systems there is not nearly as strong a conservative bias built into the interpretation methods.

It is difficult to predict what immediate impact these new testing systems will have on RFLP testing. They are much quicker to perform, but reagent and equipment costs are high, court acceptance has yet to be established, and in the case of polymarker, AMPFLPs and STRs, validation is not as extensive. It also is not clear if the level of discrimination provided by these systems is sufficient to satisfy the courts, who now are accustomed to DNA profiles of extraordinary rarity. It may be that the PCR-based methods will be used as a screening tool in investigations, elimination and plea bargaining purposes, and that in cases where there is not enough DNA to do an RFLP analysis. In cases that are not settled by the PCR results RFLP will be performed if possible.

What seems clear is that advances in PCR technology will eventually allow us to use a larger number of loci and more alleles at each locus. In the meantime, methods with increasingly greater sensitivity mean that smaller and more degraded specimens can be tested. As it did with electronics, miniaturization is beginning to revolutionize molecular biology. Scientists predict that one potential product of the fruitful union of electronics and biology might allow us to perform multiple testing of DNA upon a single silicon chip.

LABORATORY QUALITY ASSURANCE

An argument which opponents of forensic DNA frequently use is that medical labs that check to see whether or not a throat culture reveals strep are more closely regulated than forensic labs whose tests might send a man to the electric chair. In any procedure as labor-intensive as DNA analysis, particularly because the interpretation of data is required, there is the potential for human error.

Indeed, proficiency tests of 200 crime labs performed in 1978 showed an unacceptably high error rate. Tests conducted in 1988 of the three private labs doing DNA analysis showed dramatic improvement but still raised questions. The California Association of Crime Laboratory Directors sent 50 blood and semen specimens drawn from 20 people to Cellmark, Lifecodes, and Forensic Science Associates. Cellmark was wrong on one of the 44 matches it found. Forensic Science Associates erred on one of its 50 reported matches. Lifecodes had no errors, but reported matches in only 37 cases. Both errors were "operator problems," one involving a sample mix-up. These studies were done years ago and do not reflect the current state of the art and quality control.

Quality assurance is a series of procedures used by laboratories to ensure reproducibility and accuracy of results. There are three main elements to a quality assurance program:
• Inspection and certification of the laboratory;
• Examination and certification of personnel; and
• Regular proficiency testing.

Several programs are available to laboratories instituting comprehensive quality assurance programs. DNA-specific quality assurance requirements are based largely on the FBI-sponsored TWGDAM (Technical Working Group on DNA Analysis Methods) guidelines.

The American Society of Crime Laboratory Directors Laboratory Accreditation Board (ASCLD-LAB) has currently inspected and certified close to one-half of the crime laboratories in the United States. These certifications are by forensic discipline, such as DNA analysis, serology, trace evidence, and others. By the fall of 1994, there were more than 120 labs accredited, 18 of them in DNA. The American Association of Blood Banks Parentage Testing Committee also has an inspection program for parentage testing laboratories that includes a DNA certification program. The College of American Pathologists proficiency testing program tests both forensic and paternity labs. There is also a series of exams offered by the

American Board of Criminalistics that examine forensic scientists on general knowledge and then go on to test them on various specialties.

While these programs serve different segments of the forensic science community, they have similar approaches. They are comprehensive in that they perform on-site inspections of all technical operations and quality control procedures of the laboratory as well as its documentation, personnel qualification, training, security, and administrative policies.

Forensic Quality Assurance Programs

Lab Inspection and accreditation
- ASCLD (American Society of Crime Laboratory Directors) and AABB (American Association of Blood Banks)

Personnel qualifications, training, and certification
- ABC (American Board of Criminalistics) – general knowledge and specialties (*i.e.* DNA/serology)

Proficiency testing
- CTS (Collaborative Testing Services) and CAP (College of American Pathologists)

Currently, there is some debate and misunderstanding about the extent to which proficiency testing should be blind, and what can be accomplished with external proficiency testing. Fully blinded proficiency testing has been advocated as a method of determining forensic laboratory error rates and as the final arbiter of quality. This is probably impossible to consistently accomplish in a forensic context, nor is it an appropriate or cost-effective way to achieve quality control. An easy way to validate one lab's results is for a second lab to retest the evidence, only a portion of which is usually consumed by the first laboratory. An alternative is for opposing experts to observe the actual testing as part of a full review of all work done in the case.

Close and continued scrutiny of DNA, and of all forensic casework, for that matter, is essential if high quality of the work is to be maintained. Scrutiny of casework can take place after the fact by having an independent expert review all documentation, test procedures, and results. Retesting also can be performed in cases in which there is evidence left over. This often is the case because most laboratories will not totally consume an evidence stain in order to ensure that there is some left over for the opposing side to test. In cases where the evidence has to be consumed it is not uncommon for the other side to send an observer to see that the testing has been performed correctly.

Chapter 4

DNA in Parentage Testing

In the United States, establishing paternity has become a major industry. Government efforts to recover child support funds bring in over five billion dollars a year at a cost of one-and-a-half billion dollars. State and local child support agencies, working under Title IVD of the federal Social Security Act, Aid to Families with Dependent Children, administer these programs for the benefit of unsupported children. This statute requires that when a woman obtains public assistance for her children, she MUST name the possible fathers. These programs generate the bulk of almost 200,000 paternity tests performed annually. In a country where 30% of births are to single mothers, and 15% of fathers of record are

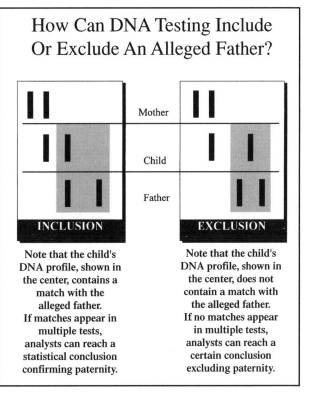

How Can DNA Testing Include Or Exclude An Alleged Father?

Mother

Child

Father

INCLUSION

EXCLUSION

Note that the child's DNA profile, shown in the center, contains a match with the alleged father. If matches appear in multiple tests, analysts can reach a statistical conclusion confirming paternity.

Note that the child's DNA profile, shown in the center, does not contain a match with the alleged father. If no matches appear in multiple tests, analysts can reach a certain conclusion excluding paternity.

not the biological father, the large number of tests is not surprising.

Parentage testing cases are numerically the largest user of DNA testing. More than 130,000 of the paternity tests performed in the United States every year use DNA testing exclusively or as a supplement to conventional blood testing. HLA (Human Leukocyte Antigen) and other classical blood typing tests often can resolve a routine paternity case without resorting to DNA testing. The HLA blood types are the types that must be matched before an organ transplant, such as bone marrow, kidney or heart, can succeed. Limitations of conventional testing are that the blood must be fresh when tested, and only a limited amount of genetic information is obtainable. Also non-blood cell types, such as those found in semen, do not have an HLA and most other common blood types, rendering this type of testing much less useful in forensic cases. The advantage of DNA testing is that many more variable genes, up to fifteen or twenty, are available. In effect, our ability to do paternity testing is no longer limited by the amount of genetic information that we are able obtain.

Most paternity testing is done for financial reasons, *i.e.*, to establish legal responsibility and provide for support. But perhaps even more important are the emotional and social issues. When testing can demonstrate conclusively to a man that he is the father of a child then he is more likely to provide not only financial support, but emotional support as well. He is more likely to bond with the child and take an active part in its life. The importance of establishing paternity early is nowhere more clearly shown than in the testing of adult children, some of whom are in middle age. "Who is my father?" is a question that often has haunted them for their entire lives.

It wasn't very long ago that obtaining a paternity test was an uncertain, expensive and inconvenient process. It was hard to find a place to have the blood drawn to initiate the testing and redraws were common as the blood had to reach the laboratory in one or two days. A doctor's or a lawyer's involvement might have been required, and, even after the effort and expense, the results often came back with a considerable degree of uncertainty. Also, there were no inspection and certification programs available to parentage testing laboratories which provide an assurance of quality.

While not as simple as getting a standard medical blood test at a doctor's office, DNA testing has made the process more convenient and the result much more conclusive. The testing is still expensive and takes several weeks to complete, but anyone can order it. In all but the rarest of instances, the DNA test results provide a level of certainty so high that paternity will, for all practical purposes, be proven or disproved.

One of the greatest benefits DNA has brought to parentage testing is the ability to solve many more types of cases. In the usual case, tests include all three parties, *i.e.,* the mother, child and alleged father. With DNA, it is not necessary to have the mother's sample in order to provide a conclusive test result. It is possible to distinguish between two brothers provided they are not identical twins. In some cases, it is even possible to perform the DNA tests when the alleged father is deceased or otherwise unavailable. It also is possible, using DNA, to perform testing before or at the time of birth. Tests also can be performed on some very unusual samples such as envelope flaps, cigarette butts, and very old blood stains.

WHAT HAPPENS AT THE BLOOD DRAW

Throughout this country, and the entire world, is a network of phlebotomists (people who draw blood) who are licensed and experienced in the legal blood draws that are necessary in paternity testing. These blood draws differ from medical blood draws by the extent to which they are documented. Clients who are

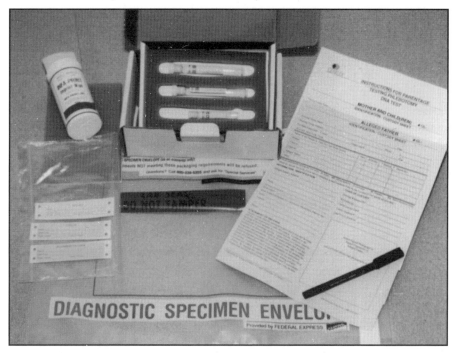

Typical parentage testing blood draw kit including chain of custody documents, blood tubes and labels for up to three individuals, approved leakproof container with absorbent materials, thumbprint supplies, tamper proof sealing tape and courier pack with preaddressed airbill.

being tested for paternity will be asked to show a picture ID, fill out and sign release forms and identification labels, and a photo or thumbprint will be taken. In this way the chain of custody (COC) that must be maintained throughout the transport and testing can be assured. In order for the COC to have maximum integrity the tested parties should not be involved in the shipping or handling of the transport kit. It should be sent directly to the blood draw site or personal physician, and include pre-addressed return airbills with instructions.

Only a small volume of blood, a teaspoon or less, will be taken in a draw. Children, even babies, usually tolerate it quite well. The blood samples from babies also are drawn from the arm because it is less painful and much quicker than a heel or finger stick. Unlike former practices, blood now can be drawn any day of the week, and all parties need not be drawn at the same time or place.

Instead of using blood, it also is possible to perform the test using a "buc-cal Swab," a Q-tip that has been rubbed on the inside of the cheek. This type of testing is likely to become more available in the future as it becomes routine and, more important, widely validated and accepted.

PARENTAGE TESTING APPLICATIONS

PRENATAL AND NEWBORN TESTING

Formerly, it was impossible to test babies until they were six months old. Testing blood from the umbilical cord of a newborn now is one of the most convenient and effective ways to obtain a paternity test. At the time of birth labor and delivery staff will take blood from the cord after the baby is born, draw the mother and ship the samples to the laboratory. Arrangements must be made in advance and if the alleged father has been drawn prior to the birth, testing can start immediately.

> **DNA Parentage Testing Applications**
>
> • Child support enforcement
> • Criminal paternity
> • Identify human remains
> • Kinship and sibship analysis
> • Medical genetics
> • Twin zygosity

One of the fastest growing areas is pre-natal testing. While it has been possible for many years to perform a prenatal test for paternity, it has not been routinely done because of the small risk to the fetus. That now is changing as the amniocentesis and chorionic villus sampling procedures are becoming more routine. These are the procedures for obtaining cells from the unborn baby which, in the past, have been limited to women over thirty-five or for families with a history of genetic disease. Occasionally, a pregnancy ter-mination decision based on the results of testing will be made. In these cases, it is recommended that accelerated testing methods be used.

DECEASED ALLEGED FATHER

This type of testing often is needed to obtain Social Security or insurance benefits, to settle an inheritance dispute or to establish standing in a wrongful death action. There are two basic approaches to solving these cases. The first is to obtain a postmortem sample of the father's DNA. The second is to reconstruct his genotype based on surviving family members. Samples from the deceased may be obtained from the medical examiner, coroner or other pathologist who may have performed an autopsy, an associated toxicology or medical lab, the funeral home before or after embalming, or even following burial for up to several years.

KINSHIP ANALYSIS – MISSING ALLEGED FATHER

If samples from the deceased are not readily available then the alleged father's genotype can be reconstructed by testing close relatives. The most straightforward of these tests is a grandpaternity test in which the alleged father's parents are tested. If one or both of his parents are missing, then samples from his siblings or other children can be used and extended typing performed. Any combination of three or four of these close relatives will result in a highly conclusive test. When fewer relatives are available for testing, the ability to provide a conclusive result decreases. Relatives farther removed from the alleged father such as cousins are not related closely enough to provide useful information. One caution to this type of testing is that if the relationships are misrepresented to the laboratory, a false negative may result.

SIBSHIP ANALYSIS

Siblings are not as closely related as parents and children. Thus it is difficult to achieve significant test results in the absence of both parents. The most difficult kinship analysis is to determine if two individuals are full or half siblings when those individuals are the only ones available for testing. If the number of siblings increase or other relatives become available, the success rate increases dramatically. It also is easier to determine if two individuals are full siblings or completely unrelated. Advanced genetic methods and powerful computers are sometimes required to solve these cases. It may be necessary to test twelve or fifteen or more genes in order to make a determination.

CRIMINAL PATERNITY

The most common and most disturbing criminal paternity cases are those involving the sexual abuse of a child. Laboratory testing is not advisable in most of these cases because the abuser is generally a relative or close friend of the family and the crime comes to light after the physical evidence is gone. Sometimes these unlawful sexual contacts do result in a pregnancy, especially if they continue over an extended period of time. In this instance, the DNA testing is usually routine and can be performed on the child or an abortus that is older than six weeks. DNA testing may be especially useful if there are closely related suspects, such as a father and son or two brothers. Criminal cases also may require the application of non-routine statistical and reporting techniques depending on the requirements of the court.

Cases where the victim of sexual abuse is underage rarely go to court. The offender usually will receive a lower prison term if he pleads guilty. Conviction in the face of DNA evidence is almost inevitable. In cases where the victim is an adult and consent is a defense, the defendant may change his story when he realizes that the DNA testing results are almost impossible to refute. The jury is usually unaware of this change of story and so often will vote to acquit the defendant.

DNA Parentage Evidence Sources
- Paternity
  Fresh blood
  Cord blood
  Abortus (within 6 to 8 weeks)
  Prenatal samples
  Saliva (buccal swabs)
- Maternity
  Abandoned, switched, kidnapped infants
- Post-mortem Identification
  Bone, teeth, heart, brain

DNA parentage testing has been questioned by the courts in only a handful of cases. Typically, less than 1 or 2 percent of civil cases result in a case contested in trial. The opportunity to have testing repeated by the same or another laboratory usually can settle most disputes to the satisfaction of all tested parties. In criminal cases, when the testing is scrutinized extensively in court, it is almost universally accepted.

GENETIC RECONSTRUCTION

These techniques often are used in homicide investigations. Suppose that there is a tissue sample from an unidentified deceased individual, or a stain from a crime scene and investigators have a good idea of the sample's source. If the decedent's parents or children are available, it will be possible to compare the related survivors' DNA profiles with that of the deceased to conclusively determine whom the remains came from.

TEST RESULTS

Paternity testing is possible because everyone has two copies of their genetic information, half from each of the parents. If a child has a gene that didn't come from the mother then it must have come from that child's biological father. If the alleged father does not have that gene, the obligate gene as it is called, then he cannot possibly be the father. He is excluded from the group of men who could be the father of the child. There is one exception. If a mutation has occurred, which means the gene changed when it was passed from the father to the child. These mutations rarely occur, but they occur often enough that two DNA exclusions are always obtained before reporting out a result.

The other possible outcome is that the alleged father has the obligate gene and so is included in the group of men who could be the father of the child. In

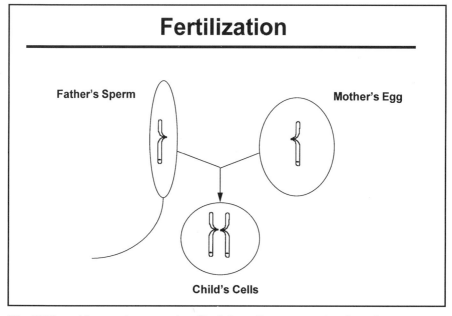

The DNA and hence the genes in all of the cells are contained in chromosomes. The bars in the three cells represents one of the 23 human chromosomes which become paired in the child's cells at the time of fertilization. This single cell will divide and grow to eventually become the adult human being.

effect, what paternity testing does is examine a series of genes until the group of men who could be the father of the child is narrowed down to the point that we can, for all practical purposes, be certain that he is the father. In DNA testing, this can be accomplished by testing as few as three highly variable genes.

PATERNITY EXCLUSION

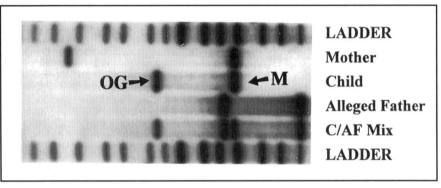

An autorad film of a paternity case DNA profile on a single chromosome. The child's gene marked M came from the mother. The other child's gene marked OG is the obligate gene. It had to come from this child's father. The alleged father in this case does not have a gene in that position, therefore, he cannot be the father of this child.

PATERNITY INCLUSION

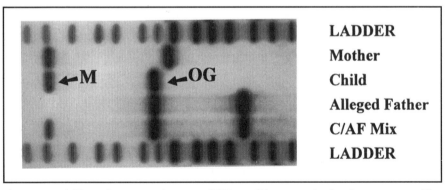

An autorad film of a paternity case DNA profile on a single chromosome. The child's gene marked M came from the mother. The other child's gene marked OG is the obligate gene. It had to come from this child's father. The alleged father in this case has a gene in that position, therefore he is included in the group of men who could be the father of this child.

Two different ways are used to report the two possible testing outcomes. An exclusion is reported as a simple statement that the alleged father is excluded from the group of men who could be the father. In the case of an inclusion, a statistical analysis is performed based on how common or rare are the obligate genes. These are the genes that the alleged father could have contributed to the child and that must have come from the child's biological father. The inclusionary results are expressed in the following two ways:

THE PATERNITY INDEX

The first is the paternity index (PI), which is a simple odds ratio. Because of the increased accuracy possible with DNA testing, the generally accepted min-

Comparative Inclusion Rates for Paternity

Paternity Index	Probability of Paternity	False Positives	Verbal Predicates Paternity:
20	95%	5%	
50	98%	1-2%	Very Likely
100	99%	< 0.1%	Extremely likely
500	99.8%	~ 0	Practically proven

Verbal Predicates, according to Joint AMA-ABA guidelines
Family Law Quarterly, Vo. X, 3,1976.

Comparison of the paternity index, probability of paternity calculated using a 50% prior chance (see text), the false positive rate for different levels of testing and the verbal predicates developed by a joint committee of the American Medical Association and the American Bar Association. The false positive rate indicates what percentage of inclusionary tests results become exclusions if further testing is done. The verbal predicates were developed to help the non-scientist understand what the numbers mean.

imum standard for an inclusionary result has risen to a PI of 100. This means that the alleged father has a 99 to 1 better chance of being the father than a random man. It does not mean that the test is only 99 percent accurate. A more realistic way to look at this result is to consider that the alleged father has a PI of 100 and that the genetic profile he must donate is found in 1 in 100 randomly chosen men. If he has been falsely accused, then he has the required 1 in 100 profile. The probability of these two events occurring together is more realistically thought of as 1 in 10,000.

DNA test results typically produce odds ratios of hundreds or thousands to one. As a practical matter, once a PI of 100 is reached, the probability of overturning that result with further testing becomes extremely small. In practice, the test results are reported out according to the race of the alleged father. While the results can vary slightly from race to race, as a practical matter, when modern DNA testing methods are used, the race of the father doesn't make a significant difference.

PROBABILITY OF PATERNITY

In the second way, the probability of paternity is calculated simply by converting the PI to a percentage. However, it can be the most confusing because the equation that is used for the calculation contains a term called the "prior probability." This term takes into account the non-genetic factors that would have a bearing on paternity. In the laboratory a neutral value of 0.5 is universally used. It favors neither the alleged father nor the mother.

The paternity index and probability of paternity represent a comparison of the alleged father against a random man in the population. If there is a close relative who also could be the father he also should be tested. If he is unavailable, then the laboratory can take that fact into account when doing the testing and calculations. Another case that the laboratory should be aware of is whether or not the alleged father is from a restricted racial or ethnic group.

CHOOSING A LABORATORY

Because paternity laboratory inspection is not mandatory, there is a wide range of quality among the laboratories. On the fringe are a number of very small laboratories which do a low volume of testing and do not subscribe to the established quality control assurance programs. In evaluating a parentage testing laboratory, one should ask if it is accredited in DNA testing by the American Association of Blood Banks. Labs may be accredited in the older types of testing, such as HLA and red blood cell testing, but not in DNA testing.

When contacting a laboratory, if it is not possible to talk with an understanding, helpful and knowledgeable client services representative, it might be advisable to look elsewhere. A lab may do fine work, but if there is not someone available to clearly explain the process and results, it can be frustrating. Another factor which can help in laboratory selection is whether or not the laboratory has provided testing and testimony in criminal cases, which require the most advanced expertise.

PARENTAGE / KINSHIP TEST RESULTS

GeneLex Corporation
2203 Airport Way South, Suite 350, Seattle, Washington 98134
Telephone: 206.382.9591 Fax: 206.382.6277

April 17, 1992

We have completed a kinship analysis on samples from the individuals listed below. Based on the scientific evidence, we conclude that it is, for practical purposes, proven that John Doe is the biological father of Baby Doe.

		Race[4]	Date Collected[1]
Mother[3]:	Jane Doe[3]	C	03/19/92
Child:	Baby Doe		03/19/92
Alleged Father:	John Doe	C	03/02/92

Laboratory # GL-1070[2]   King County IVD #000000

System	Mother	Child	Alleged Father	Paternity Index
DNA Locus[5] (Probe)[6]/Enzyme[7]				
D2S44(pYNH24)/HaeIII	2.33/1.60[8]	1.60/1.60[8]	1.60/1.32[8]	4.52[11]
D4S139(pH30)/HaeIII	8.78/5.64	8.78/3.20	9.58/3.20	44.28
D10S28(pTBQ7)/HaeIII	3.31/1.93	3.31/2.85	2.85/1.15	19.20
		Combined Paternity Index	=	3852[12]

The probability of paternity, assuming a 50%[14] prior chance is 99.97%.[13] John Doe is 3852 times more likely to be the father of Baby Doe[9] than a random Caucasian-American man.

John Doe cannot be excluded as the father of Baby Doe.

Testing was performed according to the criteria outlined in the American Association of Blood Banks Parentage Testing Standards.

T. Aulinskas [15]
Teresa H. Aulinskas, PhD
Laboratory Director

Laura J. Mendoza-Sandor, MS MT(ASCP)
Laboratory Manager

State of Washington
County of King
On this 17 day of *April*, 19 92 the named individuals personally appeared before me a notary public, and they being known to me as Laboratory Director and Laboratory Manager of GeneLex Corporation, did execute the foregoing and they did so as their free act and deed and that the same is true to the best of their knowledge and belief.
Notary Public _____   My commission expires 11-10-96

The American Association of Blood Banks Parentage Testing Committee requires that the following information be included on paternity testing reports. (The numbered items are keyed to the numbers inserted on the two sample reports).

1. The date of collection of the sample.
2. The case number assigned by the laboratory.
3. The name of each individual tested and their relationship to the child.
4. The racial origin of the alleged father used in the calculations.

GENELEX

PARENTAGE / KINSHIP TEST RESULTS

GeneLex Corporation
2203 Airport Way South, Suite 350, Seattle, Washington 98134
Telephone: 206.382.9591 Fax: 206.382.6277

April 17, 1992

We have completed a kinship analysis on samples from the individuals listed below. Based on the scientific evidence, we conclude that John Doe cannot be the biological father of Baby Doe.

		Race[4]	Date Collected[1]
Mother[3]:	Jane Doe[3]	C	02/18/92
Child:	Baby Doe		02/18/92
Alleged Father:	John Doe	C	03/19/92

Laboratory # GL-1034[2]   Jefferson County IVD #000000

System	Mother	Child	Alleged Father	Obligatory Paternal Allele
DNA Locus[5] (Probe)[6]/Enzyme[7]				
D2S44(pYNH24)/HaeIII	4.50/2.87[8]	4.50/1.58[8]	2.86/2.33[8]	1.58
D4S139(pH30)/HaeIII	8.47/4.26	7.33/4.26	9.87/7.83	7.33

John Doe is excluded as the father of Baby Doe[9] by the findings in the following systems: D2S44 and D4S139.[10]

Testing was performed according to the criteria outlined in the American Association of Blood Banks Parentage Testing Standards.

T. Aulinskas [15]
_____
Teresa H. Aulinskas, PhD
Laboratory Director

_____
Laura J. Mendoza-Sandor, MS MT(ASCP)
Laboratory Manager

State of Washington
County of King

On this _17_ day of _April_, 19_92_, the named individuals personally appeared before me a notary public, and they being known to me as Laboratory Director and Laboratory Manager of GeneLex Corporation, did execute the foregoing and they did so as their free act and deed and that the same is true to the best of their knowledge and belief.

Notary Public _____ My commission expires _11-10-96_

5. The International Human Gene Mapping Workshop name for the DNA locus tested.
6. The DNA probe used to detect the DNA locus.
7. The restriction enzyme used to cut the DNA.
8. The size of each gene fragment detected.
9. A statement as to whether or not the alleged father can be excluded.
10. The basis for an opinion of nonpaternity.
11. The individual paternity index for each gene pair.
12. The combined paternity index reached by multiplying the individual indices.
13. The percentage probability of paternity.
14. The prior chance used to calculate the probability of paternity.
15. The signature of a laboratory director who must be a Ph.D. or an M.D.

Chapter 5

DNA in the Courtroom

THE NATURE OF EVIDENCE

E vidence is any statement or material object from which reasonable conclusions can be drawn. It is a broad category embracing anything perceptible to the five senses including documents, exhibits, facts agreed to by both sides, and the testimony of witnesses. Evidence in a criminal trial concerns the intent, motive, means, and opportunity to commit a crime.

In general, evidence is divided into two categories: circumstantial and physical. Circumstantial evidence consists of information gleaned from witnesses and documents that point to an individual as the perpetrator of a crime. Physical evidence consists of actual objects - bodies, weapons, body fluid stains, fingerprints, hairs, fibers, etc. - that are associated with the crime and may be linked to the perpetrator.

It is the work of forensic scientists to examine the physical evidence, and using the methods of science, to reconstruct the events that constituted the crime. The prosecutor must then combine this data with statements of witnesses and evidence from documents such as correspondence, telephone records and credit card receipts to develop an overall theory of the case which can be presented in court.

Scientific evidence is an increasingly important part of both civil and criminal trials. Forensic science is a growth industry. New technologies for analyzing physical evidence are growing rapidly and private companies are becoming an increasingly important resource for the legal system. The testimony of experts is the primary means of introducing scientific evidence. Because these experts are imparting information "beyond the ken" of the layperson, they must present information that goes beyond first hand observation, opinions and hearsay not permitted under ordinary rules of evidence. Lay witnesses are constrained to testify only about matters they have directly observed. Expert witnesses are allowed to draw inferences from facts which the judge or jury is not competent to draw. They may also rely on seminars, publications, records and conversations with other experts that are part of their normal course of business.

DISCOVERY

Despite fictional presentations to the contrary (Perry Mason is a prime example), there are very few surprises in actual trials. This is because of the process called discovery, whereby opposing attorneys are permitted to learn the facts and expert opinions upon which the other side is basing its case prior to the actual trial. In addition, each side is required to provide the other side with a list of its witnesses before the start of trial.

Providing discovery materials in criminal cases is binding only upon the prosecution in all but a few states and Canada. Access to materials through the discovery process is the main avenue the defense has for learning what evidence will be presented against the accused at trial. This allows the defense to re-examine the evidence and develop alternative hypotheses to the prosecutor's case.

In California, the defense's access to scientific evidence is defined in the *Griffin* decision which provides that the defense can have the evidence only after the prosecution has completed their testing. Also, under both *Griffin* and a U.S. Supreme Court decision in *Arizona v. Youngblood*, the prosecution may consume the evidence in the testing process, as long as they act in good faith.

Beginning in 1989, furious battles erupted over discovery efforts in the DNA war. Generally the defense has been able to examine autoradiographs from the case in question, laboratory reports, and the lab notes that support them in addition to the lab procedure manuals and proficiency testing results. Requests for additional materials such as other autoradiographs, validation studies, population data bases, and raw data face harsher scrutiny and often were not honored. Early DNA cases were marked by long and costly litigation over discovery. The defense claims that the prosecution and the labs they employ "stonewall' discovery requests. The

---

Attorney's Discovery Request

• Primary Data
  RFLP-Autoradiographs
  PCR-Color photos of strips

• All case and bench notes
  (including chain of custody documents)

• Laboratory protocols
  (including summary of population data)

• Proficiency test results of analyst

---

lab resist discovery, maintaining that the requested materials are privileged, constitute trade secrets, are legally irrelevant.

Forensic labs also claim that the defense regularly makes overly burdensome and duplicitous requests for reams of material. If they were required to comply, lab personnel would be doing little else than identifying and duplicating discovery materials. DNA discovery battles are still being strenuously fought. Indeed, O.J. Simpson's chief lawyer, Robert Shapiro, has labeled Cellmark a "discovery outlaw." However most commentators would agree that many of the issues surrounding discovery already have been litigated or settled in other ways.

SCIENTIFIC EVIDENCE ADMISSIBILITY STANDARDS

The key element in whether scientific evidence is admissible is whether it is trustworthy. To be considered trustworthy, it must demonstrate accuracy (validity) and consistency (reliability). Admissibility is determined by the Frye rule, which stresses "general acceptance" or by the Federal Rules of Evidence (followed by some state courts) which stress helpfulness, reliability, and relevance.

In all of the trials to date in which DNA evidence has been involved, courts have ruled it as evidence or, on appeal, have remanded the case to the trial court in 22 reported cases and have limited its admissibility in 16 cases, generally because of statistical questions.

THE FRYE STANDARD

In the 1923 decision *United States v. Frye*, a District of Columbia circuit court ruled against the admissibility of lie detector evidence in a murder case because the technology had not been accepted in the relevant scientific community. Since then, most state courts have followed this general standard on whether or not to allow novel scientific evidence. The so-called Frye hearing gives the prosecution and defense the opportunity to attack adverse scientific evidence and try to keep it out of the trial. The key paragraph in this decision reads:

> Just when a scientific principle or discovery crosses the line between experimental and demonstrable stages is difficult to define. Somewhere in the twilight zone the evidential force of the principle must be recognized, and while courts will go a long way in admitting expert testimony deduced from well-recognized scientific principle or discovery, the thing from which the deduction is made must be sufficiently established to have gained general acceptance in the particular field in which it belongs.

Determining "general acceptance" according to the Frye standard is a two-step procedure: (1) identifying the particular field(s) into which the scientific principle or discovery falls and the relevant scientific community; and (2) determining whether that community accepts the technology, principle, or discovery. Both the underlying theory and the procedures used to produce results must be generally accepted by scientists in the relevant fields.

To these two criteria has been added a third in some jurisdictions. In California, the additional standard evolved from the 1976 decision in *People v. Kelly* which held that "the proponent of the evidence must demonstrate that correct scientific procedures were done in the particular case." This third "prong" also was accepted by the court in the 1989 landmark *New York v. Castro*, the first case in history of where DNA evidence was excluded. A distinction lost on some courts is that the Kelly rule only requires that correct procedures be used, not that the court must determine that these procedures were performed correctly.

Legal evidence rules generally hold that how well work is performed should not be the subject of an admissibility hearing because the quality of testing in a particular case goes to the weight of the evidence and not its admissibility. It is up to the trier of fact, the judge or the jury, to determine how much weight or consideration to give that evidence. In practice, the legal distinction between the admissibility of scientific testing and the weight that should be given that testing has become increasingly blurred in DNA evidenciary hearings.

It should be noted that, at least in California, the Frye rule does not require absolute "unanimity of views within the scientific community," which, according to the California Court of Appeals, would "demand the impossible." In *People v. Guerra* (restated in the *Reilly* case), the court ruled that, "the test is met if the use of the technique is supported by a clear majority of the members of that community." Nevertheless, some courts have interpreted "general acceptance" to mean the absence of controversy, an unrealistic standard in almost any scientific or technical area.

One result of this interpretation is that Frye hearings often last longer than many trials. The mother of all Frye hearings took place in San Diego in 1987. At issue was the methodology of pre-DNA blood typing. A personal vendetta between two experts, known as the "starch wars," exacerbated the controversy which dragged on for a full year. While courts and attorneys are often reluctant to reveal the costs of proceedings, Frye hearings are expensive.

In King County (Seattle), Washington the situation may be the worst in the country. There have been over a dozen pre-trial DNA evidentiary hearings in this jurisdiction, each requiring two to six weeks of courtroom time. Most have concerned identical technologies and laboratories. In total, these hearings are estimated to have cost the local government over $1,000,000, not counting the time that personnel such as bailiffs and guards, attorneys, experts and others have lost to more productive tasks. This might be a reasonable price to pay if the controversy had been finally settled, but at this point there is no end in sight. All costs are paid by the state in more than 90% of these cases because the defendant is indigent.

The Frye rule has been criticized for its overly conservative approach and its vulnerability to manipulation by those seeking to exclude novel scientific evidence. After the Federal Rules of Evidence were enacted, a number of jurisdictions abandoned Frye.

THE FEDERAL STANDARD

The Federal Rules of Evidence currently in force were promulgated by the Supreme Court and enacted by Congress in 1975. While they are applicable directly only to proceedings in federal courts, they serve as the model for evidence codes in 32 states. Despite this state recognition of federal standards, the majority of states profess to follow the Frye rule, creating evidenciary ambiguity that may not be resolved until appellate courts or legislatures address the issue.

While not explicitly repudiating the Frye rule, the Federal Rules adopt a more permissive approach. They liken the standard for scientific evidence to that for other evidence, *i.e.* whether the probativeness, materiality, and reliability of the evidence outweighs its tendency to mislead, prejudice, and confuse the jury. The judge has more discretion under the Federal Rules.

Rule 702, which concerns admissibility, states:

> if scientific, technical, or other specialized knowledge will assist the trier of fact to understand the evidence or to determine a fact in issue, a witness qualified as an expert by knowledge, skill, experience, training, or education, may testify thereto in the form of an opinion or otherwise.

Rule 703 requires that the facts or data presented be "of a type reasonably relied on by experts in the particular field." Rule 403 excludes evidence that would cause undue prejudice or confusion. Proponents of the Federal Rules approach to admissibility believe that taken together, these rules address all the concerns embodied in the Frye rule.

DAUBERT V. MERRELL DOW

Critics of the Federal Rules fear that the courts may be opening themselves to "junk science" by relaxing Frye, but a landmark case heard by the Supreme Court in 1993 rejected that claim. In *Daubert v. Merrell Dow Pharmaceutical, Inc.*, the court unanimously held that the Frye rule was incompatible with and had been superseded by the adoption of the Federal Rules. It found that "vigorous cross-examination, presentation of contrary evidence, and careful [jury] instruction are the traditional and appropriate means of attacking shaky but admissible evidence." Trial courts also could still render summary judgments and directed verdicts where there was an insufficient showing of reliability.

Frye Standard

General Acceptance of Theory and Practice

Federal Rules

Helpful

Relevant

Reliable

Daubert

Emphasizes Judicial Discretion

The effect of *Daubert* on states where rules mirror federal standards has yet to be felt. However, it is reasonable to assume that expert testimony on DNA will be admissible after a threshold finding that it is relevant and reliable. Defendants in these jurisdictions will have a harder time suppressing DNA evidence, although stiff challenges to its admissibility will undoubtedly continue, at least for the near future. *Daubert* will have little or no effect on states where Frye still prevails. Some of the states even have supreme court decisions affirming Frye. The most recent state to affirm Frye is California in the Leahy case, decided in October 1994. In these states, new high court decisions or legislation are the only means to change admissibility standards.

LEGISLATED ADMISSIBILITY

By the Fall of 1994, eleven states had statutes mandating the admissibility of DNA evidence. Maryland became the first state to do so followed by Minnesota, Louisiana, and Nevada, all in 1989. Most of the legislation contains language that DNA testing is acceptable "without antecedent expert testimony" that it is "a trustworthy and reliable method." Arguably, these laws do not cover DNA analysis methods introduced after their passage, and the defense may still challenge laboratory performance and the statistical interpretation of results. As a more sophisticated defense bar mounts increasing numbers of expensive challenges to DNA evidence, it is likely that additional state legislatures will address this issue.

EXPERT WITNESSES

While many expert witnesses represent the best in their profession, the proliferation of expert witnesses, often considered to be "hired guns" employed to shoot holes in the other side's testimony, is a remarkable development in the criminal justice system. There is hardly any kind of case not affected by these duelling experts, but psychological, medical, and DNA testimony seems to bring out the worst of them. It is difficult not to conclude that some of these individuals are willing to stretch or ignore the facts, distort the science, and become "liars for hire." Many of these witnesses derive a substantial amount or even the bulk of their income from testifying, which should be considered in determining their credibility and weighing their testimony. One California judge bemoaned the use of such witnesses by candidly calling them the beneficiaries of "a welfare system for academics."

A recent article on the ethics and responsibility of expert witnesses suggests the following criteria for qualification:
- Undergraduate and graduate degrees in the relevant field of expertise;
- Specialized training in the subject area as it relates to forensic science;
- Some training in forensics;
- Professional licenses or certifications required by professional groups in the expert's discipline;
- Evidence of experimentation, teaching, and publication within the specialty area; and
- Prior disciplinary evidence directly relevant to the issues being considered.

Other elements that help to determine an expert's qualifications include: post-graduate training, publication in peer-reviewed scientific journals, the development of accepted tests and procedures, membership or leadership in appropriate scientific societies, and, only lastly, experience as an expert witness.

Ten years ago the Califonia case *People v. Brown* added criteria that has proven difficult to apply, ie., that the witness "must also be 'impartial,' that is, not so personally invested in establishing the acceptance of a technique that he might not be objective about disagreements within the relevant scientific community." Neither should a witness be so invested in denigrating a technique that he exaggerates the disagreement within the scientific community. Probably the best way of gaining the testimony of impartial witnesses is for courts, rather than litigants, to appoint and pay for expert witnesses. Such is the practice in many other countries. While it is unusual in the U.S, this procedure is within the power of state and federal courts. A notable example in a case involving DNA was *United States v. Yee*, where the magistrate called Eric Lander, a mathematician-turned-geneticist, as an expert witness to supplement the seventeen expert witnesses called by the prosecution and defense. It is reported that Judge Ito may call his own expert witnesses during the Simpson case Kelly-Frye hearing.

DEFENSE STRATEGY

Defense witnesses mount various objections to DNA evidence. They no longer try to discredit the technology itself. Years ago, DNA typing achieved such wide acceptance and proven reliability that opponents now concentrate on two principal points of attack: (1) the quality and methodology of the laboratory work, including the lab's error rate, and (2) the statistical interpretation of data. The focus of the attacks on admissibility have changed over time. As one objection was knocked down, DNA opponents came up with another. The quality and relevancy of the arguments and of the experts is decreasing, having gone from population geneticists to bio-statisticians to statisticians from completely unrelated fields. What follows is a summary of the most frequently heard complaints about DNA typing and the responses to them that might be expected from forensic scientists. More technical objections, such as bandshifting and laboratory quality assurance, are addressed in Chapter Three.

CONFLICT OF INTEREST

Prosecution and defense expert witnesses in DNA cases are arguably the most contentious and disparaging in the business. Several judges have remarked that Frye hearings over DNA can be extremely vicious. Among the charges and countercharges hurled back and forth is that the opposing witnesses should be disqualified from testifying because of a conflict of interest. To a certain extent, both sides are correct. The prosecution believes that defense witnesses in DNA hearings often have a vested interest in making sure that the subject stays controversial so that they can continue the lucrative practice of testifying. The defense often believes that a practicing forensic scientist has a built-in bias or predisposition toward the prosecution's side because of the close working relationship between crime labs and law enforcement. Indeed, criminalists often are police employees.

If the forensic scientists are leaders in their field, they may be subject to a further conflict of interest. If they have developed or invented techniques or tools, they may have a proprietary interest in advancing DNA testing. They may have financial holdings in DNA labs or may have received grant funding from public or private agencies. Certainly, a jury is entitled to know about all of these connections which should be fully disclosed. At the same time, courts acknowledge that, "simply because learned experts earn a living with their expertise

Lines of Attack on Forensic DNA Testing

General
  No Quality Assurance Required of Labs
  Conflict of Interest of Experts
  Personnel not Adequately Trained
  Insufficient Materials Provided in Response to Discovery

Chain of Custody
  Documentation not Adequate
  Samples Improperly Stored or Transported
  Not all People/Technicians Who Handle Evidence are Testifying
  Fraud or Evidence Tampering Committed

Technical
  Lab Procedures not Followed Correctly
  Contamination Prior to or Following Evidence Submission
    Mixed Stains
    Non-Human DNA Present
    Other Substances Inhibitory to Testing
    PCR Product
  Samples Switched Inadvertently
  Band Shifting and Ethidium Bromide
  Inadequacy of Validation Studies
  Procedures not Peer-Reviewed

Statistical
  Population Studies not Adequate
  Inappropriate Database Used
  Undetected Substructure Excessive
  Product Rule not Applicable
    Locus does not Follow Hardy-Weinberg
    Loci are in Linkage Disequilibrium
  Database not Adequately Tested or Peer Reviewed
  Error Rate not Known or Incorporated into Calculations

should not prohibit the admissibility of their opinions," as the court ruled in a recent New Jersey case.

INTEGRITY OF SPECIMEN

Opposing expert witnesses try to raise doubts about the way DNA evidence was gathered and tested claiming that contamination may have occurred. The usual argument is that the underlying procedures for forensic DNA testing were developed in laboratories where pure and known samples were used and retesting always was an option. While this is true, the argument doesn't mention the usual results of contamination, the ease with which it can be detected, and the safeguards that are in place in most forensic DNA labs.

In almost all cases, the results of using a specimen sufficiently contaminated to alter test results simply would be ruled inconclusive. One way a specimen might be contaminated is by genetic material from the technician performing the analysis or from the person gathering the evidence. Again, this could not possibly harm the accused as an exclusion would be the result of such mishandling. Finally, there is the possibility that some of the DNA drawn from the suspect could be accidentally mixed with DNA retrieved from the crime scene. Such an accident would yield false results, especially if PCR amplification is used. To avoid this possibility, crime labs that perform PCR do it in isolation and under stringent conditions that minimize the risk of contamination.

DNA analysis is undeniably better than other tests in analyzing mixed specimens and overcoming a variety of contaminants. Because of its structure and relative stability, DNA can be tested even after mixture with acids, bases, gasoline, oil, or bleach.

ERROR RATE

The newest objection, which is at the heart of the Simpson defense team's argument to exclude DNA evidence, is the testing lab's error rate. In a field as complicated as forensic science there are many sources of error, most of which will lead to an inconclusive or no result. A false positive or negative error rate is impossible to measure because these are such rare events. These are the types of errors caused by human error or fraud. It should be noted that most of these types of mix-ups or failures in the chain of custody would lead to a false negative result which would be work in the accused's favor. These also are more likely to occur before the evidence is received by the laboratory. There is no rate of these kinds of errors that is acceptable. Fortunately, an error resulting in a miscarriage of justice has yet to be demonstrated in forensic DNA casework, although it is perhaps inevitable that it will occur someday.

Errors intrinsic to the testing systems, such as the inability to precisely measure DNA restriction fragment lengths, are well compensated for by interpretation guidelines which take these kinds of errors into account. The series of quality control steps built into the process also provide an excellent assurance of the quality of individual and laboratory performance. In most cases these steps should lead to corrective action long before a catastrophic error has occurred.

Minimizing laboratory errors requires a quality control program such as the ones which already are in place on a voluntary basis in the forensic laboratories. Almost all forensic DNA laboratories participate in programs which include proficiency testing and confirm that a minimum level of performance has been achieved. External proficiency testing also provides an ongoing comparison of inter-laboratory measurement error. These programs, led by the American Society of Crime Laboratory Directors Laboratory Accreditation Board are rapidly gaining momentum.

In the forensic field, the final arbiters of quality are the courts where experts under examination and cross-examination submit their results to the scrutiny of the opposing experts and the judge and jury. This added level of scrutiny is necessary to ensure quality forensic work and includes review of casework, retesting, and observation of particular tests by opposing experts. Both sides need to have equal access to forensic expertise in the interests of fairness and justice.

POPULATION GENETICS ESTIMATES

The most contentious debate in forensic DNA involves the use of statistics to estimate the rarity of a given DNA profile. This is to be expected because the extraordinary rarity of these profiles is what gives them their conclusiveness as evidence. The rarities of the genetic profiles depend on the number of genes examined (usually four or five, often more). The frequencies of the results of each gene are multiplied to reach a combined profile frequency or the final estimate which is presented to the court.

Critics contend that among certain ethnic sub-groups, there may be arrangements of gene frequencies that differ markedly from those found in the general population. They maintain that the population base used to give frequency statistics must be drawn from the suspect's particular gene pool, i.e., if a suspect is half Vietnamese and half French, the population database used to compute the probability ratio must reflect this ethnic mix.

This argument depends on the premise that there are significant differences in gene frequencies between ethnic groups and that a suspect should be compared only to genetic peers when calculating the likelihood that someone else could share the suspect's DNA profile. Why the pool of potential assailants must match the suspect's ethnicity is difficult to fathom. In any case, studies have shown that all populations have similar gene frequencies. While the frequencies might vary slightly, the differences are insignificant, especially when averaged over several genetic loci. Additionally, it now is clear that the differences within population groups are greater than the differences between them. Perhaps most importantly, the systems used to calculate frequency estimates are inherently conservative. They are designed to be biased in favor of the suspect and more than compensate for any slight differences between sub-populations.

FALSIFICATION OF EVIDENCE

News "leaks" and other statements indicate that the Simpson defense team is making charges of official misconduct and falsification of evidence in the case. This is an accusation seldom made in regard to any kind of evidence. Nevertheless, because it will probably be raised by the Simpson defense team, and because there have been some recent, flagrant examples of forensic misconduct, this claim needs to be considered.

In the Fall of 1994, a case arose involving a San Francisco police lab technician, Alison Lancaster. After co-workers became suspicious about her reports, Lancaster was the target of an internal sting operation. She was provided with samples of non-drug specimens which she identified as heroin and cocaine. As many as 1,000 cases may have been compromised because Lancaster worked on them. The full extent of her falsification may never be known because in many cases the evidence she "tested' was subsequently destroyed.

Perhaps the most notorious case of falsifying evidence in contemporary America involves Fred Zain, a long time West Virginia state police officer and crime lab "magician," most recently employing his talents in Texas. Zain now has been indicted for perjury and tampering with evidence. Several hundred cases are affected, and two men, one convicted of murder and the other of rape, already have been released and compensated.

There is no case on record where DNA evidence has been falsified.

THE TRIAL

In terms of DNA, the actual trial often proves to be anti-climactic. Presumably most of the fireworks have been shot off during the evidentiary hearing, especially if testing results are presented. Sometimes this hearing is basically repeated during the trial. But, in a surprising number of cases, once the DNA is admitted, the defense declines to call its witnesses back again during the trial. A substantial number of cases involving DNA never reach the trial stage because suspects plead guilty after the identifying results are ruled admissible. Another common occurrence in rape trials, if the defendant has lost the admissibility hearing, is for him to change his story and claim the sex was consensual. The jury will usually not be aware of this change.

```
┌──────────────────────────────────────────────────┐
│              Levels of Proof                     │
│ • Civil:    Substantial evidence                 │
│             Clear and convincing                 │
│             Preponderance of evidence (>50%)     │
│                                                  │
│ • Criminal:  Proof beyond a reasonable doubt     │
│                                                  │
│ • Scientific: Proof to a scientific or medical certainty │
└──────────────────────────────────────────────────┘
```

A key concept to bear in mind during any legal case is the burden of proof or level of persuasion required to find a defendant guilty. The lowest level of proof is found in administrative hearings and the like where "substantial evidence" is sufficient. The fact finder need not even be convinced. He or she must merely not be unconvinced by the evidence. The next level of proof is "clear and convincing evidence," and is commonly employed in civil fraud cases.

Other civil cases, including paternity suits, are determined by a "preponderance of evidence." The trier of fact must find more than half the evidence supports a claim before it can be deemed true. The highest burden of proof is required in all criminal cases, where the prosecution must prove the defendant guilty "beyond a reasonable doubt." Forensic evidence can provide "scientific certainty" which should remove any and all reasonable doubts.

Previous case law determines how judges must rule in certain circumstances. They are bound to follow applicable precedents from earlier cases involving similar sets of facts or legal issues. This is what makes the appeal process so very important.

THE APPEAL

In 1988, Florida became the first state to affirm on appeal the use of DNA in the cases involving Tommy Lee Andrews, a rapist. Despite noting that the evidence was "highly technical, incapable of observation, and required the jury to either accept or reject the scientist's contention that it can be done," the appellate judges allowed the lower court decision to stand.

Maryland became the next state to uphold DNA admissibility and other related issues. Kenneth Cobey had been convicted of rape and appealed the decision, contending that (1) the single-locus probe used by the lab was not accepted by the scientific community, (2) their population data base was insufficient, and (3) his Fourth Amendment rights were violated when a blood sample was drawn from him. In 1989 The Court of Special Appeals rejected all of Cobey's arguments.

In the Summer of 1989, in three unanimous rulings the Virginia Supreme Court upheld the capital murder and rape convictions of Timothy Spencer, affirming that the DNA testing was reliable and admissible evidence. In January 1989 the U.S. Supreme Court refused to hear Spencer's appeal.

It was not until November 1989 that a high court ruled DNA evidence inadmissible. The Minnesota Supreme Court was satisfied that DNA tests, when properly performed, were admissible, but was not convinced that Cellmark had produced reliable test results. The court was troubled by Cellmark's one incorrect match in the proficiency test conducted by the California Association of Criminal Laboratory Directors. They also found that Cellmark did not meet proper guidelines such as formal methodology validation recommended by the FBI.

Since then, DNA has found wide and general approval by the courts, with occasional exclusions. By October 1994, 117 federal and state appellate courts and state courts of last resort had ruled in favor of admitting RFLP evidence. Fourteen state high courts had accepted the evidence with reduced or no statistics, and twenty appellate level courts had excluded the evidence or remanded the case to trial court for resolution. PCR testing has not established as lengthy a record. There have been a total of ten decisions in PCR cases and all have ruled in favor of admitting the DNA evidence.

CALIFORNIA APPELLATE DECISIONS

California intermediate appellate court decisions on DNA evidence are unanimous in accepting the theory and methods of RFLP testing. However, several courts differ in their rulings on the admissibility of the statistical interpretation of the data. The first of these is the 1991 Axell ruling which admitted both the testing and the interpretation. Less than a year later, Judge Ming Chin threw out the statistical estimates which had been used in *People v. Barney*. Judge Chin ruled that since the time of Axell, opinions in the scientific community had changed regarding the statistics and population genetics of DNA testing and that there now existed a controversy where none had existed before. He stated that the controversy was generated by an article in Science magazine and by the release of the National Research Council report on forensic DNA which recommended the "interim ceiling principle."

Two other relevant decisions followed in short order: *People v Pizzarro* and *People v. Wallace*. The *Pizzarro* case was remanded to the trial court for additional evidence on gene frequencies. In *Wallace*, the court rejected the DNA evidence for statistical reasons, but affirmed the conviction and claimed that the error was harmless. This also is the finding in six of the seven cases heard since then. The California Supreme Court thus far has refused to rule on any of the DNA cases, most likely because the lower courts affirmed the convictions in all of the cases except the two remanded for further hearing. How much longer California appellate courts will be able to avoid dealing directly with the question of DNA admissibility while hiding behind the claim of harmless error is a good question. Perhaps the Simpson case will make the issue too big for the courts to ignore.

As this book goes to press the California 4th District Court of Appeal unanimously upheld the use of DNA evidence in a rape trial. Calling DNA evidence "highly reliable and relevant" the court upheld the conviction of Frank Lee Soto. The appeals court also ruled that the frequency calculations provided by the prosecution met general acceptance in the scientific community. While the ruling has no direct bearing on the Simpson case because it is being tried in a different jurisdiction, it is inevitable that Judge Ito will take notice of this decision.

POST-CONVICTION RELIEF

One of the highest and best uses of DNA in the criminal justice system is to free people who have been mistakenly identified by an eyewitness (often the victim), wrongfully convicted, and incarcerated. To date, about a dozen men have had convictions reversed and been released from prison thanks to latter-day DNA testing.

A recent case involved Frederick Rene Daye who was arrested for the kidnapping, robbery, and rape of a San Diego woman in 1984. The victim positively identified Daye, and despite several exonerating elements, he was convicted. DNA testing had not yet been used in court at the time of Daye's trial. Once the validity of genetic testing was established, Daye, who had always maintained his innocence, requested DNA analysis of the crime evidence and a California court of appeals granted his request.

The results which came back from a private lab in April 1994 excluded Daye as the assailant. Despite this finding, the district attorney and trial court refused to reopen the case. After considerable pressure from a San Diego television station which got behind the cause of freeing Daye, the district attorney ordered his own retest which also exonerated Daye. After these results were returned in September 1994, Daye was released after 10 years in prison.

Two organizations have led the effort to discover and rectify past injustices through present day DNA testing: Centurion Ministries and the Innocence Project. Two principals in the Innocence Project are Peter Neufeld and Barry Scheck, co-chairs of the National Association of Criminal Defense Lawyers DNA Task Force and members of the Simpson defense team. Despite their ardent advocacy of DNA testing when it favors the accused, Scheck and Neufeld propose a moratorium on its use by the prosecution.

DNA: A LAW UNTO ITSELF?

DNA evidence has been treated differently from virtually all other forensic evidence by some courts. Stricter admissibility standards are applied to DNA as some judges require that all issues in dispute be resolved before any evidence is presented to the jury. Under the spell of DNA, these jurists seem compelled to become amateur scientists while allowing scientists to act as legal advisors to the detriment of both science and the law.

The result of this confusion and lack of uniformity by the courts over admissibility has led to a situation where the same piece of DNA evidence might be treated differently in each different venue. In the face of this inconsistency and in concluding any arguments about the validity and admissibility of DNA evidence, four telling points must be emphasized:

- There has never been a false positive (match or inclusion) DNA test in a court case on record. Nobody has ever been convicted by DNA evidence and later exonerated;
- There has been only one example of an apparent false negative (non-match or exclusion) DNA test in a court case on record. With this possible single exception, nobody has ever been excluded as a suspect by DNA and still convicted of the crime with which he was charged;
- Even when DNA evidence was not admitted, almost every defendant identified by DNA either has pled or was found guilty; and
- No retest of DNA evidence in a court case has ever resulted in inconsistent conclusions from the original analysis.

SUPERIOR COURT OF THE STATE OF WASHINGTON - COUNTY OF KING

THE STATE OF WASHINGTON,)
)
               Plaintiff,)   No. 93-1-00489-0   NOV 1 6 1993
)
          vs.)
)   AFFIDAVIT OF
)   DR. ERIC S. LANDER
Keith Dyer,)
)
_____Defendant._)

AFFIDAVIT BY CERTIFICATION:

The undersigned certifies that the following is true and accurate.

1.   I am Dr. Eric S. Lander.

2.   I am a Member of the Whitehead Institute for Biomedical Research, Professor of Biology at the Massachusetts Institute of Technology, and Director of the Whitehead Institute/MIT Center for Genome Research. I was a member of the Committee on DNA Technology in Forensic Science, impaneled by the National Research Council of the National Academy of Sciences. I served on the Advisory Panel on Forensic Uses of DNA Tests for the U.S. Congress Office of Technology Assessment. I chair the Genome Research Review Committee for the National Center for Human Genome Research. I have served on numerous other committees of the National Institute of Health. I have served on the Editorial Boards of many publications, including <u>Genomics, Human Mutation, Mammalian Genome, Theoretical Population Biology, BioTechniques, PCR Methods and Applications, Current Opinion in Genetics & Development, Genetic Epidemiology, Human Molecular Genetics, Genetic Analysis: Techniques And Applications (GATA)</u> and <u>Computational Biology</u>. I received my Ph.D. from Oxford University, was a Rhodes Scholar and have been awarded a MacArthur Fellow for research in human genetics. My curriculum vitae is attached to this Affidavit and incorporated herein.

3.   I have been qualified as a scientific expert concerning DNA Technology for Forensic Applications in <u>New York v. Castro</u> (called by the defense) and <u>U.S. v. Yee</u> (called by the court, as a court's witness).

4.   DNA typing evidence, utilizing RFLP technology, is a useful and powerful tool for identifying suspects in criminal cases.

5.   The application of population genetics to DNA typing must be held to a high standard of science. In my opinion, it is possible to meet this standard in a legal setting by using evidence in a conservative fashion. It is with this goal in mind that the NRC adopted the ceiling principle and interim ceiling principle methods for calculating population frequencies.

Experts who do not actually testify in person to a court can make their views knows through affidavits.

6. DNA fingerprinting evidence and its statistical interpretation, prepared and presented in court in accordance with the criteria set out in the NRC report, meet the high standard of science and is generally accepted within the community of population geneticists.

7. Specifically, estimating population frequencies in accordance with the interim ceiling principle is a standard of practice so conservative that no serious scientific argument based on data could be made to say that such an estimate could be biased against the defendant. Although there remains considerable scientific debate concerning the best estimate of the true population frequency, there is general acceptance that the modified ceiling principle provides an under bound to the true frequency.

8. I have read the court's opinion in State of Washington v. Hollis in which the court excluded evidence of a DNA identification. As a scientist, the court's analysis is troubling to me. The court focuses on the fact that scientists disagree about the best method of estimating population frequencies, but seems to miss the point that scientists can disagree about the best estimate of a frequency, while agreeing that a formula (or even several alternative formulas) provide an upper bound on the frequency. This is the case for the interim ceiling principle, which makes adequate allowance for variation among populations and results in estimates that would not overestimate the case against the defendant.

I declare under penalty of perjury under the laws of the Commonwealth of Massachusetts that the foregoing is true and correct.

Dated this 20th day of September, 1993, at
Cambridge, Middlesex County, Massachusetts

_____

Eric S. Lander, Ph.D.

Signed and sealed before me, this 20th day
of September, 1993

_____
Christina R. Whalen
My Commission Expires: February 3, 2000

Chapter 6

DNA and O.J. Simpson: The Trial of the Century

At no time in history has someone as well-known and well-liked as O.J. Simpson been accused of such a heinous crime as slitting his ex-wife's throat, almost decapitating her, and the knifing to death of her friend who happened on the scene. For the American public, obsessed as it is with celebrity, the Simpson case is proving to be a riveting spectacle. As this book goes to press in December 1994, the trial itself has yet to start and but every legal proceeding except for jury selection has been broadcast live, covered thoroughly, and analyzed exhaustively.

There is no escaping the Simpson trial. Management consulting firms are predicting that once the trial starts, an epidemic of "Simpsonitis" is going to lower productivity in the American workplace. The case is the staple of television and radio shows, articles, editorials, and commentaries, jokes, and cartoons. Even Doonesbury has assigned several characters to cover the trial and they are staying in a "big media encampment called O.J. City." The case is being used as the basis for law classes at Harvard, Yale, U.C.L.A. and several other law schools (O.J. 101). The trial will be broadcast on ESPN, the all-sports cable network. It is likely that by the time the trial is over, it will have received more news coverage than any event since the Viet Nam War.

As part of this media frenzy, DNA typing, the crucial evidence in the case, is receiving unprecedented attention. To people in the forensic sciences, this attention is greeted with the hope that the Simpson case will be the acid test for DNA in the courts, at least in the court of public opinion. At the same time, there is some concern that the defense is mounting the most concerted and well-funded attack ever on DNA evidence. Will they succeed in confusing the judge or the jury? The dollars versus DNA showdown at the Simpson evidentiary hearing and the trial will be a real test of the criminal justice system.

The pre-trial hearing, called the Kelly-Frye hearing in California, where the judge will decide on the admissibility of the DNA testing was initiated by the defense motion to exclude the DNA evidence. That document was submitted on October 5 and runs 108 pages. The motion is well written and goes back to the beginnings of DNA testing to cite a wide variety of articles, affidavits, and testimony which challenge the validity of DNA. It quotes two Nobel laureates, one of whom will testify for the defense that the PCR test is not suitable for forensic use. This motion was rebutted by two documents from the prosecution, one asking the court to admit the RFLP testing and the other PCR.

It is highly unusual for jury selection to precede the Kelly-Frye hearing, as was done in the Simpson case. Both sides usually want to know the outcome of the hearing prior to selecting a jury because the judge's ruling on admissibility affects the way in which they question prospective jurors. Judge Ito did not really have a choice in this case, however. All of the DNA test results were not yet back from the laboratories, so the full extent and kinds of evidence could not yet been determined. At this stage, an evidentiary hearing would have been able to address only generic and not specific issues.

The Kelly-Frye hearing, originally scheduled for Nov. 1, and then Dec. 12, 1994, has now been postponed until January 5, 1995 at the earliest. Even this date might prove unrealistic because Peter Neufeld, co-counsel of the Simpson DNA defense team, is tied up with a murder trial in New York. Another unrealistic expectation is that the Kelly-Frye hearing will only take a month. Between 20 and 30 witnesses have been identified. If they averaged two days of testimony apiece, a two to three month hearing would ensue. In addition to defense and prosecution witnesses, Judge Ito may call his own experts to testify. If he does, Eric Lander from M.I.T. is bound to be one of them. Ito is being advised on DNA issues by Judge Dino Fulgoni, a Los Angeles Superior Court judge and former prosecutor specializing in DNA issues.

Both sides did get some early insight into how prospective jurors felt about DNA evidence. As part of jury selection, all members of the jury pool were required to complete a 78-page questionnaire probing their views on such subjects as race, religion, sports, politics, science, and, of course, DNA. Of the 294 questions, the eight dealing with DNA are printed at right.

The jury that was chosen for the Simpson case is composed of eight African-Americans, two Hispanics, one American Indian-Caucasian, and one Caucasian. Four are men and eight are women. The jury includes two people with more than a high school education. Based on their questionnaires, the Simpson jury, by and large, does not find DNA evidence to be reliable.

In the Simpson case, it is a victory for the defense to have the jury selection come first. The longer the jury sits, the more chance there is for a mistrial, especially if the jury is sequestered. Every time there is a mistrial, it is a victory for

---

JUROR QUESTIONNAIRE
XV. DNA
The ability of DNA analysis to prove the identify of the person(s) whose blood or hair is found at a crime scene has been the subject of some television and radio shows, and magazine and newspaper articles.

The following questions pertain to this subject.

193.   Before the Simpson case, did you read any book, articles or magazines concerning DNA analysis?

If yes, please name the book, magazine, newspaper or other periodical where you read about it and briefly describe what you recall having read.

194.   Since the Simpson case, have you read any articles concerning DNA analysis?

If so, please indicate in which magazine or newspaper you read those articles and briefly describe what you recall having read.

195.   Are you aware of any other court cases involving DNA analysis?

If yes, please describe these cases as completely as possible and state what you recall about them and the role DNA analysis played in the outcome.

196.   What is your view concerning the reliability of DNA analysis to accurately identify a person as the possible source of blood or hair found at a crime scene?

____Very reliable ____Not very reliable____ Don't Know

____Somewhat reliable   ____Unreliable

197.   Have you followed any court hearings concerning DNA analysis in the Simpson case?

If yes, please check all the media sources that apply:

Note: A list of Television, Radio, Newspaper, Magazine and Tabloid sources followed.

198.   From these sources, how much would you say you have heard about DNA analysis in the Simpson case?

199.   What do you recall hearing and/or reading about the DNA hearings in the Simpson case?

200.   What are your views concerning what you have heard and/or read about the DNA hearings in the Simpson case?

---

the defense even though the prosecution more often than not convicts the next time around.

Judge Ito was probably thinking about the length of the trial and the potential for "contamination" of the jurors by the media when he decided to qualify twelve alternate jurors instead of the more usual eight. Judge Ito probably realizes that the Kelly-Frye hearing may well last considerably longer than the month for which it is currently scheduled, and that the trial itself may run far longer than anticipated. Because both sides believe that alternate jurors will be used in this case, seating of the alternate jurors took longer than choosing the original panel.

DEFENSE STRATEGY AND ARGUMENTS

The defense began their DNA offensive by waging a pitched battle to convince Judge Ito to split the blood evidence samples in the Simpson case. This was a tactical move to reduce the amount of DNA available to be tested by the prosecution. The defense probably doesn't want to do any testing of its own because it would only add a fourth lab to the three which have already processed incriminating evidence against their client. They want to distance themselves from this evidence so much that they did not even observe the testing which was done. The most productive avenue for the defense in this case is to discredit the evidence by criticizing how it was collected and documented on its way to the lab. To embellish this argument, they claim that the "contaminated" samples are unfit for re-testing.

Beginning with the pre-trial evidentiary hearing, the defense will try their utmost to blur the distinction between weight and admissibility so they can talk about issues such as laboratory error rates and contamination. These relate more properly to the weight of the evidence rather than to its admissibility. Ideally, the defense would like to have the scientists who did the testing testify about the results. They will reach far into the past to bring up any statements, cases or tests which support their position.

The attacks the defense will make are based on trying to show that DNA testing is not reliable and that there is no agreement in the scientific community as to how the results should be interpreted. Statistical estimates and population genetics, especially as they relate to RFLP, are still a major defense objection despite the fact that many of the experts who previously expressed concerns about the population genetics issues will no longer testify against the forensic use of DNA. This issue is further neutralized by the recent article in Nature co-authored by Bruce Budowle and Eric Lander.

Laboratory error rate is the most recent area that the defense has emphasized to try to keep DNA out of the courtroom. This is actually an old issue. While there is no particular case law on this point, it is generally considered to go to the weight of the evidence irrespective of the testing method. By error rate in the DNA context, critics are referring to the incidence of false positive test results. The basic defense contention is that until the laboratories can establish their false positive rates by double blinded proficiency testing, they should not be allowed to use the test results as evidence.

Based on proficiency testing that the laboratories underwent years ago, defense experts have calculated that false positive rates could be as high as 30%. This is a specious claim. It assumes that the occurrence of false positives in forensic casework follow the rules of statistics used for normal distributions of frequently occuring events. False positive results in the laboratory are extraordinarily rare events. Out of the more than 25,000 cases which have been completed using forensic DNA, not one false positive result has been demonstrated to date.

The defense will bring up the results of a 1987 test in which both Cellmark and Forensic Science Associates reported out false results. They will claim that these test results point to a lab error rate of 2% (1 in 50 tests). These tests are irrelevant because changes in protocols were made as a result of these tests and since then many thousands of tests have been sucessfully completed. The defense is also claiming that the laboratory error rate should be factored into any DNA profile frequencies so that the gene frequencies reported could never be any lower than the false positive rates. Once again, this is an inappropriate use of statistics, because the occurrence of a genotype and the occurrence of an error are two different events.

Much will be made of the procedural errors made in the Simpson case, particularly the coroner's performance. Those errors, while certainly demonstrating substandard performance, are not material. The time of the victims' death is known with much greater certainty than can be determined by discarded stomach contents. The failure to collect sexual assault evidence is disappointing but, of course, there are no allegations or evidence of sexual assault. Often, there are much more serious breaches of investigative procedures, but few defendants have the resources that are available to O.J. Simpson.

The defense objections to the DNA evidence are summarized in the following excerpt of their motion to exclude DNA evidence.

ROBERT L. SHAPIRO
State Bar No. 043693
GERALD F. UELMEN
State Bar No. 39909
SARA L. CAPLAN
State Bar No. 147271
BARRY C. SCHECK, ESQ.
State Bar No. 62646
PETER J. NEUFELD, ESQ.
WILLIAM C. THOMPSON, Ph.D.
State Bar #104967
Law Offices of Robert L. Shapiro
2121 Avenue of the Stars
19th Floor
Los Angeles, CA 90067
310/282-6255; 310/553-3000

Attorneys for Defendant,
ORENTHAL JAMES SIMPSON

FILED
LOS ANGELES
SUPERIOR COURT

OCT 05 1994

EDWARD M. KRITZMAN, CLERK

BY _____, DEPUTY

SUPERIOR COURT OF THE STATE OF CALIFORNIA
FOR THE COUNTY OF LOS ANGELES

THE PEOPLE OF THE STATE OF CALIFORNIA, --against-- ORENTHAL JAMES SIMPSON, aka O.J. SIMPSON Defendant.	Case No. BA097211 MOTION TO EXCLUDE DNA EVIDENCE In Department 103, Los Angeles County Superior Court

TO THE CLERK OF THE ABOVE-ENTITLED COURT AND TO THE DISTRICT
ATTORNEY OF THE COUNTY OF LOS ANGELES:

Defendant, ORENTHAL JAMES SIMPSON, by and through counsel,
hereby moves this Honorable Court for an order providing that:

I. Pursuant to the rule in People v. Kelly (1976) 17 Cal.3d
24, 130 Cal.Rptr 144. governing the admissibility of scientific
evidence, the results of forensic DNA testing the prosecution
intends to introduce at trial be excluded on the following grounds:

A. The statistical estimates being offered for Cellmark's RFLP, polymarker, and DQ Alpha tests, DOJ's D1S80 and DQ Alpha tests, and LAPD's DQ Alpha tests should not be admitted because the statistical methods used by the laboratories are not generally accepted as reliable, i.e., there is an ongoing controversy in the relevant scientific communities (statisticians and population geneticists) where experts significant in quality and quantity object to the reliability of the methods. The issues in controversy include:

1. The general acceptance of the methods used to determine the probability of a coincidental match for each test (RFLP, polymarker, D1S80, and DQ Alpha);

2. The general acceptance of the methods used to determine the false positive error rates of the laboratories for each test;

3. The general acceptance of methods used to express the probability that the defendant is the source of DNA evidence: whether it is appropriate to express the probabilities of a coincidental match and a false positive error as one statistical estimate, two statistical estimates, or in some other fashion;

B. The reliability of the methods used by the LAPD, Cellmark, and DOJ for collecting, handling, processing, and testing crime scene samples for forensic use of each PCR based test (DQ Alpha, D1S80, and polymarker testing).

The issues in controversy include:

1. The general acceptance of the methods used by crime scene LAPD investigators and laboratory analysts to prevent the contamination of crime scene samples given the uniquely sensitive nature of PCR based DNA testing;

2. The general acceptance of subsequent testing of crime scene samples given the failure of the LAPD laboratory to document and control sources of PCR contamination in its laboratory;

3. The general acceptance of using each of the PCR test (DQ Alpha, D1S80, and Polymarkers) to analyze forensic crime scene samples;

II. Pursuant to California Evidence Rule Section 352, DNA statistical estimate should not be presented to the jury because, given the present state of the controversy over coincidental match probabilities and false positive error rates, to do so would be unfairly prejudicial, confusing, and misleading. The issues in controversy which should engender unfair prejudice and confusion include:

1. Overstating the value of DNA evidence by

(a) Failing to present one statistical estimate to the jury which combines the probability of a coincidental match and the false positive error rate of the laboratory; or

(b) Failing to provide just the comparatively high false positive error rate of a test when the coincidental match probability is much lower;

2. The controversy over the validity of methods for calculating the probability of coincidentally matching DNA profiles;

3. The controversy over the validity of methods to determine the false positive error rate of a laboratory for a particular technique;

III. Pursuant to People v. Griffin (1988) 46 Cal.3d 1011, DNA results from crime scene samples should not be admitted because in the collection, preservation, and processing of crime scene samples LAPD crime scene technicians and laboratory personnel failed to preserve them properly, thereby making subsequent testing by other laboratories unreliable.

THE DEFENSE DNA TEAM

Barry Scheck and Peter Neufeld are the two American attorneys best known for their DNA defense work. This pair from New York has been at the middle of the muddle over DNA since the first big showdown in New York v. Castro. They followed that case by forming the DNA Task Force of the National Association of Criminal Defense Lawyers, which they continue to co-chair. Then they handled the DNA hearing in U.S. v. Yee. Now they're involved in the Simpson trial.

At a recent international DNA symposium, they were reviled in a joking aside by one speaker as the "princes of darkness." Peter Maas, the best-selling writer, describes his two friends by saying, "Scheck is short and pugnacious; Neufeld is tall and pugnacious." Both are known as hard workers who take on a lot of civil liberties cases and pro bono work. Through the Innocence Project, the two have used DNA testing to free several innocent men who were serving time for crimes they did not commit. Scheck and Neufeld, who are in their mid-forties, first came together as Legal Aid "people's lawyers" in a South Bronx ghetto.

Scheck is a professor at Yeshiva University's Cardozo School of Law, where he also directs a criminal law clinic for students. Neufeld is a private practicioner in Manhattan and also teaches law at Fordham University. In December 1994, Neufeld found himself in trouble as he tried to withdraw from a murder trial in New York so that he could devote his full attention to the Simpson case. The New York judge found that Neufeld's declarations "bordered on" perjury and threatened him with contempt and jail if he dropped his east coast client to seek his "fame and fortune" in California. A federal judge also rejected his plea to be removed from the New York case.

William Thompson is an associate professor of criminology at the University of California, Irvine. He has a Ph.D. in psychology and a law degree from Berkeley. Thompson was largely responsible for writing the motion to exclude the DNA evidence and is an excellent writer. His article on lessons from the "DNA War" published in Northwestern University's Journal of Criminology and Criminal Law has become a favorite primer for critics of DNA testing. Thompson's academic commitments may prevent him from having much more involvement in the case.

DEFENSE EXPERTS

The first two experts retained by the defense are widely known and highly respected among forensic scientists. Henry C. Lee is a native of China and, before coming to this country, was a police officer in Taiwan. He now serves as the head of the Connecticut State Police crime laboratory and is a longtime advocate of DNA testing. Lee is an expert in crime scene investigation and blood spatter interpretation. He has investigated more than 5,000 murders, solving a number of difficult homicides, including the infamous case in which a man attempted to dispose of his wife's body by dismembering it with an industrial woodchipper. By arrangement with the State of Connecticut, he is permitted to do private work. He testified, for example, as a defense witness in the William Kennedy Smith rape trial in Palm Beach, Florida. Lee has Governor Weicker's explicit permission to work on the Simpson case. He went to California shortly after the arrest of Simpson and visited the crime scene. He has also been to the Los Angeles Police Department lab to view the evidence.

Ed Blake is the other forensics expert who has worked for the defense from the beginning. He is the founder of Forensic Science Associates, a private lab in California. He has been to the California State Crime Lab in Berkeley frequently and has also visited the Maryland lab and the LAPD lab. Blake is one of the original practicioners of forensic DNA testing in the country. In fact, in 1986, he performed the first DNA testing ever allowed into a courtroom in the United States. Blake was the object of a prosecution subpoena, but Judge Ito refused to issue the subpoena, saying that it was not necessary to have Blake's direct testimony since he has published widely and his views can be ascertained from his writings and his testimony in the scores of previous trials in which he has testified in favor of DNA testing.

Ironically, the defense may decide to not put either of their two top forensic experts on the stand. With the prosecution barred from seeking their testimony, neither Henry Lee nor Ed Blake is likely to be seen at the Kelly-Frye hearing or the trial itself.

Simpson's lawyers delayed submitting their list of witnesses. Rumor suggests that the defense had a difficult time locating desirable witnesses to testify on their behalf. High profile academics such as Lewontin and Hartl, who have testified for the defense in the past, are now satisfied that forensic DNA methods are acceptable. Indeed, Hartl will testify for the prosecution. The defense bar, more and more has been forced to call individuals who are only tangentially qualified to testify on forensic DNA matters.

Prior to being qualified by the judge to give expert testimony each witness will be examined and cross examined in a process called voir dire, from the French "to speak the truth." On cross-examination by the opposing attorneys during voir dire, as well as for the remainder of the hearing, and during the trial a constant goal of the attorneys will be to discredit the opposition's expert witnesses. Attorneys will review transcripts of previous testimony; published and unpublished documents such as articles, grant applications, copies of manuscripts and related correspondence for inconsistencies and ammunition. Anything the attorneys can get their hands on by legal means is fair game, including what are normally treated as confidential matters. The attorneys will bring up questions of conflict of interest, how much money the witnesses have made, if they have testified only for one side, and their outside employment. If judges did not live in such fear of being overturned on appeal they probably would not qualify some of these individuals as experts.

The defense hopes that their main witness, Kary Mullis, will be an ace-in-the-hole, the high trump card that allows them to win the showdown. He is, after all, a Nobel laureate who won his prize by inventing the PCR testing process that the prosecution is using to help prove Simpson's guilt. Although Mullis has already testified in a handful of DNA cases, he can be considered a coup for the defense because the Nobel Prize is so prestigious. He will testify that PCR testing should not be used for identifying criminals.

At the same time, Mullis might backfire on the defense, his views are so often rejected and ridiculed by the scientific community. In Nature magazine for example, Robin Weiss, director of the British Institute of Cancer Research, compared Mullis to William Shockley, who won his Nobel for inventing the transistor. Shockley is most famous for his views that whites are intellectually superior to blacks. While Mullis' views are not racist, they too are offensive to scientists.

He believes that AIDS is spread through the lungs, not sexual contact or shared needles, and that HIV does not cause AIDS. He also believes in a conspiracy linking the "government" and the Mafia, which has targeted O.J. Simpson and aims to bring him down with faked evidence.

Based on his previous testimony, Mullis does not appear to be familiar with the controls which are used in forensic PCR tests that prevent and detect contamination. Indeed, Mullis is largely unfamiliar with current lab practices. He no longer practices science, having abandoned that career to try his hand at writing. His only connection to PCR now is that he hopes (through his company called Stargene) to market pieces of jewelry or trading cards containing PCR-generated DNA from Madonna, Elvis Presley, and other famous personalities.

Seymour Geisser is a biostatistician and the (co)author of about 150 technical articles. For more than twenty years, he has been a professor and the director of the school of statistics at the University of Minnesota. He has testified in dozens of trials as a defense witness against DNA. In previous testimony, Geisser has maitained that the data base upon which DNA frequency estimates is based must be drawn from the geographic area in which the suspect resides.

Elizabeth Thompson chairs the statistics department at the University of Washington, although this year she is on leave at the University of Michigan. A native of Great Britain, Thompson is new to testifying, having only one previous experience (the Hollis case in Seattle, Washington). There she was instrumental in getting the DNA evidence ruled inadmissable. A Seattle lawyer familiar with her testimony in the case observed, "the prosecution often accuse the defense of hiring whores, but Elizabeth was a virgin."

William Shields is a professor of biology and the director of the Cranberry Lake Biological Field Station for the State University of New York at Syracuse. A zoologist by training, he wrote his Ph.D. dissertation on inbreeding and the evolution of sex in birds. His specialties are orinthology and testifying for the defense in DNA cases.

Laurence Mueller is a professor in the Department of Ecology and Evolutionary Biology at the University of California, Irvine. Along with William Thompson (who wrote the motion to exclude DNA evidence for the Simpson team) and Simon Ford, a DNA consultant no longer at the university, the trio became known as the "combine from Irvine" for their prolific work challenging DNA. Mueller has a Ph.D. in ecology and wrote his dissertation on fitness in fruit flies. He has the distinction of earning more money through witness fees than any other veteran of the DNA War.

THE PROSECUTION DNA TEAM

There are three prosecutors working on the DNA aspects of the case. The lead is Lisa Kahn, the Los Angeles County DNA coordinator since 1990. She is particularily interested in the technical and scientific aspects of the subject and has attended numerous scientific conferences on forensic DNA testing. Kahn frequently trains and advises other attorneys on the subject. After some early sparring with Barry Scheck over the DNA testing, Kahn was forced to limit her involvement in the case because of the impending birth of her first child due in December.

While the Scheck-Kahn exchanges were of limited duration, they were marked by deep animosity. In a tactic reminiscent of George Bush continually mis-pronouncing the name of Saddam Hussein, Kahn repeatedly referred to Scheck and Neufeld as "Schecht" and "Newfield." Scheck was theatrical with frequent grimaces of disgust and disdain and a barrage of charges and reasons why the prosecution should be sanctioned or penalized. Judge Ito admonished both attorneys for their obnoxious behavior. The length of time that jury selection has taken and the holiday recess may allow Kahn to again enter the case during the Kelly-Frye hearing.

If not, Kahn will be replaced by George Clarke and Rockne Harmon, two highly-experienced DNA prosecutors who have already assisted in the case. They were largely responsible for writing the briefs answering the defense motion to exclude the DNA evidence. Harmon, an Alameda County Deputy District Attorney, wrote the RFLP brief. He has published widely on DNA in the popular and scholarly press, especially about admissibility issues. Harmon, whose parents named him after the legendary Notre Dame football coach Knut Rockne, is known as the lawyer's lawyer on DNA. He has advised prosecutors all over the country. In his own jurisdiction, he works with police and other investigators at the earliest possible point to ensure the fullest and best use of DNA evidence.

George Clarke, who is with the San Diego County District Attorney's training division, is responsible for the PCR brief. He is the de facto DNA coordinator for his office. Clarke was the prosecutor in the longest-running Frye hearing in history, California v. Lucas, 1987-88. He is a frequent lecturer and one of the top experts on California scientific evidence case law. Clarke has the distinction of being one of the few attorneys to make a scientific contribution to an international conference on DNA. He demonstrated how a lab tried to have substandard DNA work entered into evidence.

PROSECUTION EXPERTS

During the Kelly-Frye hearing, the prosecution will probably lead off with Bruce Budowle. With a Ph.D from Virginia Polytechnic Institute, he became the FBI's chief DNA researcher and architect of the Hae III RFLP system and of D1S80, a newer kind of test. While Budowle has never performed forensic testing himself, he has testified extensively on behalf of the FBI since well before the advent of DNA testing. He has been a frontline combatant in the DNA war and will testify to the validation studies which have been performed under FBI auspices. Budowle also will likely testify about the five volume worldwide population study on RFLP that the FBI has compiled. He will speak to the validity of the private Maryland lab's testing methods as they are somewhat different from those used in almost all of the other forensic DNA labs in North America.

Ranajit Chakraborty will testify for the prosecution on statistical issues. Chakraborty is a professor of population genetics, biometry, and human ecology at the University of Texas, Houston. As a young man studying in his native India, he became interested in human genetic diversity long before it became a question in forensic science. His 1970 Ph.D. dissertation was a statistical analysis of population sub-structure. He has continued these studies and has performed considerable research on genetic variation both on DNA and non-DNA genetic systems. He received a National Institute of Justice grant to study genetic variation in forensic RFLP systems and so he will be criticized for having a conflict of interest. He concludes that less than one percent of the genetic variation seen between forensic DNA profiles is due to population variation, and that the rest (more than 99%) is due to individual variation.

Henry Ehrlich will testify to the validity and development of the various PCR tests especially the DQA and Polymarker tests. Ehrlich has been employed, first by Cetus (the company that introduced PCR), and since it was taken over, by Roche. He has been in charge of the use of PCR in human genetic testing since 1986. The DQA test is based on his detailed characterization of this gene in the mid-1980s. Ehrlich is a former colleague of Kary Mullis.

Rebecca Reynolds is also a longtime employee of Cetus/Roche and began the development of the Polymarker test while a post-doctoral fellow in forensic science at the University of California in Berkeley. She will testify about the newer methods of preforming DNA tests. Both Erlich and Reynolds are former colleagues of Kary Mullis.

Daniel Hartl, is a former opponent of forensic DNA and star defense witness. He carried weight testifying against DNA, because he and Richard Lewontin with whom he frequently teamed, are two of the more prominent population geneticists in the world. Hartl, formerly the head of the statistics department at Washington University in St. Louis, has now joined Lewontin at Harvard. He will testify about population genetics and the validity of methods used to calculate frequency estimates.

Robin Cotton is the laboratory director of Cellmark Diagnostics, the private testing lab in Germantown, Maryland that is performing DNA tests for the prosecution in the Simpson case. She will be able to address the certification questions put to her by the defense because last summer Cellmark became the first non-governmental DNA lab in the U.S. to earn accreditation from the American Society of Crime Lab Directors-Laboratory Accreditation Board.

Bruce Weir, a British native, is a professor of statistics at North Carolina State University. Weir literally wrote the book on evaluating genetic data. His Genetic Data Analysis is considered to be the definitive study of the field. He will testify about population statistics.

Brad Popovich, a medical geneticist at the Oregon Health Sciences University, will testify about DNA typing outside the forensic setting. He will address PCR testing, specifically its applications and validity.

Michael Conneally is an Irish native and a professor of medical and molecular genetics at the University of Indiana School of Medicine. He has (co)authored some 350 articles or papers, many on genetic linkages and population data bases. He will testify about population genetics and frequency estimates.

PROSECUTION STRATEGY

The prosecution will want to separate the pre-trial evidentiary hearing into two parts: one to deal with RFLP testing and the other to deal with the PCR-based tests. Although there is some overlap of witnesses, each technology has a different basis and legal history. The prosecution will call several witnesses on each subject who will describe the theoretical basis for the testing, related medical and other uses of similar testing, and the forensic validation and use of the technology.

The prosecution will try to define the scope of the hearing narrowly and draw a very sharp line between admissibility and weight. This is signaled by the fact that they may not call any witnesses from the laboratories who did the actual work in the case. The initial testimony will be confined to the soundness of the theory underlying the testing and the ability to reduce it to practice.

Detailed testimony on how statistics and population genetics are used to make an estimate of the significance of the DNA profiling data will likely be saved for rebuttal. Some of the best prosecution experts, such as Chakraborty, may be saved for rebuttal. In this way the prosecutors can answer the defense's population genetics and statistics objections based on what the defense actually says. Some prosecutors will make the error of putting on these arguments in anticipation of what the defense arguments will be. This is always a mistake because it puts the defense in a much better position to frame the issues.

	Nicole Simpson-Brown Item #59	Ronald Goldman Item #60	O.J. Simpson Item #17	Item #49 Photo ID #114
ABO	A	ind O	A	ind A
EsD	1	1	1	1
PGM Sub-type	1+	2+1+	2+2-	2+2-

Frequency of Occurrence of Combined Genetic Marker Types Identified in Item #49 = 0.43% or approx. 1 in 200

A comparison of blood from the two victims and the suspect and the drops of blood leading away from the scene (Item #49).

The prosecution's strategy must focus, in part, on the defense efforts to discredit the blood evidence and those who gathered it or analyzed it. With so much evidence in the prosecution's hand, the defense faces a stiff challenge.

The trail of blood drops next to the footprints leading away from the murder scene has been demonstrated by DNA testing to be consistent with O.J. Simpson's. If some of the blood in the Bronco, broken into or not, could be linked to Ron Goldman or Nicole Brown, or if Nicole's blood is found on Simpson's clothing or in his shower drain, that would be damning evidence indeed. Potentially, the most incriminating evidence is the bloody glove found on the Simpson estate. Several combinations are possible. The worst for Simpson would be if it contained blood from all three parties.

The prosecution reportedly has over 70 pieces of evidence, much of it blood-related, which tie Simpson to the killings. By conventional blood typing (which eliminates more than 99% of the general population) the blood of Simpson, Goldman, and Brown-Simpson are distinguishable. Without the money and fame of O.J. Simpson, there would be little need to do DNA testing in this case. There are many killers serving time in prison on much less evidence than is available to the Simpson prosecutors.

CONCLUSION

Judge Ito is not bound by appeals court rulings outside his own jurisdiction, but a November 22, 1994 decision from California's Fourth District may presage Ito's opinion on the defense arguments against DNA.

The case arose from Frank Lee Soto's conviction of attempted rape of an elderly woman who suffered a severe and totally debilitating stroke after the attack, rendering her incapable of testifying. The best evidence of the crime was a semen stain on the woman's bed spread that matched a blood sample taken from the defendant. Soto challenged the admissibility of the DNA, specifically attacking the methods used to calculate the likelihood of a random DNA match.

Soto maintained that the "product rule" used to calculate frequencies was inaccurate, because it failed to consider population sub-structuring. The article by Hartl and Lewontin from Science magazine was introduced to support this contention. Since the Soto case was tried, other significant DNA cases in California and other states have been tried and appealed, the National Research Council issued their DNA study, and Lander and Budowle published their blockbuster article in Science. The Fourth District Appeals Court took all these developments into consideration in reaching their unanimous opinion.

Several of the expert witnesses in the Simpson case testified in the Soto case and the appellate court took issue with those representing the defense, finding them irrelevant. Their ruling states that "Drs. Mueller, Geisser, and Shields are not human population geneticists, the 'relevant, qualified scientific community' for this subject: Mueller is a professor of ecology whose genetic research was limited to fruit flies; Dr. Geisser is a biostatistician whose work was limited to mathematical use of statistics; and Dr. Shields is an environmental science professor whose genetic work principally dealt with nonhuman population concerns." In contrast, the court found Ranajit Chakraborty, who will testify for the prosecution in Simpson, to be qualified and persuasive.

The Fourth District Appeals Court affirmed the conviction of Soto. In addition, it found the product rule and methods derived from it, such as the ceiling principle, to be accepted by the scientific community. It rejected the arguments of Laurence Mueller and his colleagues and accepted the arguments of Ranajit Chakraborty and his colleagues. It dismissed the idea that there had to be unanimity or the absence of controversy in the scientific community before DNA evidence is admitted. In short, it found the forensic use of DNA to be "highly reliable and relevant."

Judge Ito would do well to follow the lead of the Fourth District Appeals Court.

POST SCRIPT: On December 13, 1994, the day this book went to press, the Simpson defense team sprung a surprise. They requested that the pre-trial evidentiary hearing to determine the admissibility of the DNA evidence be waived. By doing so, they did not waive their right to challenge the evidence; they simply wish to postpone their challenge until the jury can be present.

The supposed aim of this motion is to speed up the trial, and it would unquestionably accomplish that. A recent Kelly-Frye hearing in another California double murder, *People v. Wynn*, began in August 1994 and did not conclude until early December, and there were many fewer witnesses than are scheduled in the Simpson case. The Simpson evidentiary hearing could have lasted equally as long and cost several hundred thousand dollars. Faced with the fact that Judge Ito would probably admit the evidence, Simpson's lawyers beat a strategic retreat and avoided another pre-trial setback.

The Simpson team may well be laying the ground for an appeal by hoping that they can, in essence, conduct the Kelly-Frye hearing in front of the jury and thoroughly confuse them. Indeed, in their motion to exclude the DNA evidence, Simpson's lawyers note that since "scientists, lawyers, and judges have considerable trouble engating and following these debates, how can a jury in this kind of circumstantial case be expected to do so given the current level of controversy?" If the Simpson team can later prove that the DNA evidence was simply beyond the comprehension of the jury, that it was more prejudicial than probative, they could win an appeal.

How Judge Ito will respond to this latest and most dramatic ploy remains to be seen. Whether he grants the motion or not, however, it is certain that the ultimate showdown over DNA will unfold in Los Angeles. . . sooner or later.

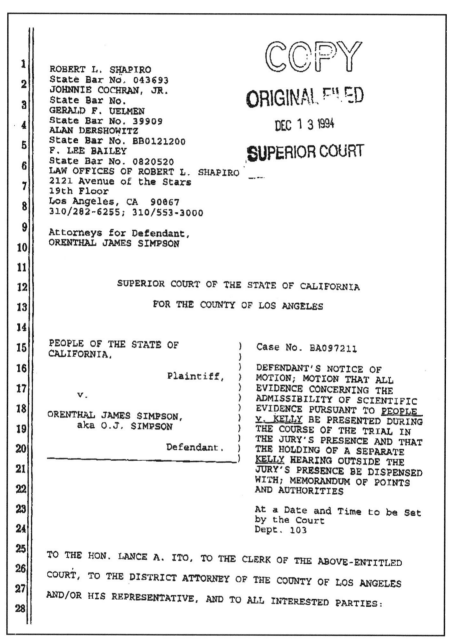

1 ROBERT L. SHAPIRO
   State Bar No. 043693
2 JOHNNIE COCHRAN, JR.
   State Bar No.
3 GERALD F. UELMEN
   State Bar No. 39909
4 ALAN DERSHOWITZ
   State Bar No. BB0121200
5 F. LEE BAILEY
   State Bar No. 0820520
6 LAW OFFICES OF ROBERT L. SHAPIRO
   2121 Avenue of the Stars
7 19th Floor
   Los Angeles, CA 90067
8 310/282-6255; 310/553-3000

9 Attorneys for Defendant,
10 ORENTHAL JAMES SIMPSON

ORIGINAL FILED

DEC 1 3 1994

SUPERIOR COURT

11

12   SUPERIOR COURT OF THE STATE OF CALIFORNIA

13   FOR THE COUNTY OF LOS ANGELES

14

15 PEOPLE OF THE STATE OF   )   Case No. BA097211
    CALIFORNIA,   )
16   )   DEFENDANT'S NOTICE OF
                      Plaintiff,)   MOTION; MOTION THAT ALL
17   )   EVIDENCE CONCERNING THE
        v.   )   ADMISSIBILITY OF SCIENTIFIC
18   )   EVIDENCE PURSUANT TO PEOPLE
    ORENTHAL JAMES SIMPSON,   )   v. KELLY BE PRESENTED DURING
19   aka O.J. SIMPSON   )   THE COURSE OF THE TRIAL IN
)   THE JURY'S PRESENCE AND THAT
20   Defendant.)   THE HOLDING OF A SEPARATE
    _____)   KELLY HEARING OUTSIDE THE
21   JURY'S PRESENCE BE DISPENSED
                                      WITH; MEMORANDUM OF POINTS
22   AND AUTHORITIES

23   At a Date and Time to be Set
                                      by the Court
24   Dept. 103

25 TO THE HON. LANCE A. ITO, TO THE CLERK OF THE ABOVE-ENTITLED

26 COURT, TO THE DISTRICT ATTORNEY OF THE COUNTY OF LOS ANGELES

27 AND/OR HIS REPRESENTATIVE, AND TO ALL INTERESTED PARTIES:

28

The Simpson Team surprised court watchers with an eleventh hour request to incorporate the admissibility hearing into the trial itself.

Afterword

A QUESTION OF JUSTICE

The prospects for ending the DNA War quickly are dim, unless the Simpson trial delivers a knockout blow to the critics. (Any decision in the case is guaranteed to be appealed, although a mistrial is a likely initial result.) The process of having an admissibility hearing for practically every case involving DNA ensures continuing contention. Standards are changing, but changing such hoary procedures is seldom either easy or quick, especially when entrenched interests find them lucrative.

The forensic use of DNA should be of special interest to women. Few commentators have identified it as such, but DNA testing is not just an ethical, legal, or public policy issue; it is also a women's issue. Ninety percent of the the victims of crimes involving DNA identification are committed against women. The tests are most useful in sex crimes, traditionally the toughest to solve and among the most under-reported. Only about half of the reported rapes result in arrests, and less than half of the men arrested are convicted. DNA has made it a lot harder for violent offenders to prey on women with impunity.

While the debate over DNA has taken some decidedly nasty turns lately, it helps to remember that there were controversial elements about DNA testing from the beginning. Civil libertarians feared abuses and voiced concerns over violations of privacy and due process.

We can also better understand the future of DNA fingerprinting by recalling the history of digital fingerprinting. A similar debate, with identical questions took place a century ago. Could more than one person have the same print? Would investigators take care in gathering the evidence? Could they fake the evidence? Now as then, as Daniel Koshland, the editor of *Science*, has observed, "caution is appropriate; unreasonable doubt is not."

The DNA revolution has brought into sharp focus how hard it is for the judicial system to evaluate and incorporate new scientific technologies. Its vulnerability to pseudo experts is exposed. Such controversies over DNA as do exist speak more to the nature of our legal system and the politics and economics of the scientific community than to the soundness of the technology, the state of the art and science.

Perhaps the recent United States Supreme Court's Daubert decision, which encourages judges to exercise greater latitude in evaluating new scientific evidence, will help to resolve the remaining admissibility questions. Appellate decisions affirming DNA testing and legislated admissibility are two other means of resolution.

Ultimately, complete acceptance of current and meritorious new DNA methodologies is inevitable, as these analytical tools will simply become even more powerful than they are today. In the meantime, we should not defer the use of such a tool for justice while we wait for the perfect solution to all questions that it raises. We must not forego good way of interpreting the results of DNA testing because there is still (and probably always will be) debate over the best way to interpret them.

Justice deferred is justice denied, and DNA has a lot to do with justice: for thousands of victims of assault, murder, and rape and their families; for the 1000 men, mistakenly accused and exonerated annually by DNA; for the approximately 3,500 criminals convicted every year, in part, by DNA evidence; and finally, justice for a nation whose citizens are safer because DNA is a powerful weapon against violence.

Appendix

DNA Decisions in the United States

ALABAMA

First Case: People v. Perry, guilty of rape, Scottsboro, 1988
Appellate Decision: Accepted DNA, remanded Perry to trial court on basis of statistics and three-pronged Frye standard, 1991; trial court found general acceptance of statistical analysis, 1992.
Data Bank established:1994
Legislated Admissibility passed: 1994

ALASKA

First Case: DNA evidence accepted in criminal trial in Kodiak, 1990.
Data Bank established:no
Legislated Admissibility passed: no

ARIZONA

First case: People v. Bible, Superior Court judge ruled to allow the introduction of DNA evidence in the murder trial of Richard Bible. Bible was charged with murder, kidnapping, and child molestation in the disappearance and death of a 9-year-old girl. Coconino County, 1989.
Appellate Decision: People v. Bible, 1993. DNA evidence admitted, but statistical estimates excluded.
Data Bank established: 1990
Legislated Admissibility passed: no

ARKANSAS

DNA evidence was admitted in a Little Rock rape case following a pretrial hearing in November 1989.
Appellate Decision: Prater v. Arkansas, 1991. Affirmed DNA admissibility.
Data Bank established: no
Legislated Admissibility passed: no

CALIFORNIA

First case: People v. Axell, guilty of murder, Ventura County Superior Court, 1989.
Appellate Decision: People v. Soto, 1994. Affirmed admissiom of evidence and statistics.
Data Bank established: 1990
Legislated Admissibility passed: no

COLORADO

First case: People v. Gallagher, guilty of sexual assault, El Paso County, 1988.
Appellate Decision: Fishback v. State of Colorado, 1993. Admitted DNA evidence and left statistical frequency questions to trial courts.
Data Bank established: 1990
Leglislated Admissibility passed: no

CONNECTICUT

First case: People v. Williams, PCR test conducted fails to show link between defendant and woman stabbed to death in a shopping center parking lot, Stamford, 1989.
Appellate Decision: State v. Silvri, 1994. Judgment reversed and case remanded with recommendation to conform with NRC report.
Data Bank established: 1994
Legislated Admissibility passed: 1994Delaware
First case: People v. Pennell, guilty of murder, Wilmington, 1989.
Data Bank established: 1994
Legislated Admissibility passed: 1994

DISTRICT OF COLUMBIA

First case: Green v. District of Columbia, After being convicted in June, 1989, Green pursued DNA testing, which revealed that he was not the individual whose semen had stained the victim's clothing. Rape, kidnapping, and sodomy charges dropped in 1990
Appellate Decision: U.S. v. Porter, 1994. Affirmed admissibility and use of ceiling principle.
Data Bank established: no
Legislated Admissibility passed: no

FLORIDA

First case: People v. Andrews, guilty of rape, 1987.
Appellate Decision: Toranzo v. Florida, 1992. Affirmed admissibility and frequency estimate.
Data Bank established: 1990
Legislated Admissibility passed: no

GEORGIA

First case: People v. Redding, DNA evidence admitted after pretrial hearing in rape case. Defendant pleaded guilty. Decatur, 1988.
Appellate Decision: Morris v. State, 1994. Affirmed use of evidence and statistics.
Data Bank established: 1992
Legislated Admissibility passed: no

HAWAII

First case: People v. Manning, guilty of assault and burglary, Wailuku, 1989.
Appellate Decision: State v. Montalbo, 1992. Admitted DNA evidence and found objections regarding statistical calculations go to weight rather than admissibility.
Data Bank established: 1992
Legislated Admissibility passed: no

IDAHO

First case: People v. Horsley, guilty of rape, Sandpoint, 1988.
Data Bank established: no
Legislated Admissibility passed: no

ILLINOIS

First case: Case of Gary Dotson. Cook County judge vacates 1979 rape conviction after DNA test exculpates defendant. Dotson had been convicted in a 1977 rape, for which he spent 6 years in jail. Alleged victim recanted story in 1985, and Governor James Thompson granted clemency, but rape conviction remained on his record. Dotson had requested that the case be reopened for new trial after PCR tests excluded him. Cook County, 1989.
Appellate Decision: People v. Lipscomb, 1991. Accepted DNA tests and statistical calculations.
Data Bank established: 1990
Legislated Admissibility passed: no

INDIANA

First case: People v. Hopkins, guilty of rape/sodomy/ murder, Fort Wayne, 1989.
Appellate Decision: McElroy v. State, 1992. Court upheld DNA admissibility and frequency calculations.
Data Bank established: 1990
Legislated Admissibility passed: 1991

IOWA

First case: People v. Vargason, guilty of sexual abuse, Johnson County, 1989.
Appellate Decision: State v. Ripperger, 1994. Affirmed use of evidence and statistics.
Data Bank established: 1990
Legislated Admissibility passed: no

KANSAS

First case: People v. Pioletti, guilty of murder, Wichita, 1988.
Appellate Decision: State v. Wilson, 1991. Ruled that procedural questions related to weight of evidence rather than admissibility.
Data Bank established: 1991
Legislated Admissibility passed: no

KENTUCKY

Appellate Decision: Harris v. Commonwealth, 1992. Affirmed the use of DNA evidence and statistics.

Data Bank established: 1992
Legislated Admissibility passed: no

LOUISIANA

First case: People v. Quatrevingt, guilty of murder/rape, New Orleans, 1990.
Appellate Decision: State v. Quatrevingt, 1992. Ruled DNA evidence is pro se admissible under Louisiana statute.
Data Bank established: no
Legislated Admissibility passed: 1990

MAINE

First case: People v. McLeod. The prosecution, in sexual molestation case, withdrew DNA evidence during a preliminary hearing on the reliability of the data, Portland, 1989.
Data Bank established: no
Legislated Admissibility passed: no

MARYLAND

First case: People v. Tasker. Defendant pleads guilty to second-degree rape and draws 5-year prison sentence in case where DNA evidence introduced. Anne Arundel County, 1988.
Data Bank established: 1994
Legislated Admissibility passed: 1991

MASSACHUSETTS

First case: People v. Curnin, guilty of rape, Worcester, 1989.
Appellate Decision: Commonwealth v. Daggett, 1993. The supreme court, unable to reach consensus on the admissibility of DNA evidence, ruled that even if the evidence was erronously admitted, it was a harmless error.
Data Bank established: no
Legislated Admissibility passed: no

MICHIGAN

First case: People v. Fagan, guilty of rape, Flint, 1988.
Data Bank established: 1994
Legislated Admissibility passed: no

MINNESOTA

First case: People v. Nielson, guilty of murder, Ramsey County, 1989.
Appellate Decision: State v. Johnson, 1993. Upheld admissibility of DNA evidence including frequency statistics for each individual locus and not the product of all loci.
Data Bank established: 1990
Legislated Admissibility passed: 1989

MISSISSIPPI

First case: People v. Weaver, guilty of rape, Hinds County, 1989.
Appellate Decision: Polk v. State, 1992. Court found 3-prong Frye standard satisfied and evidence properly admitted.

Data Bank established: from and after January 6, 1996.
Legislated Admissibility passed: no

MISSOURI

First case: People v. Thomas, guilty of rape, St. Louis, 1989.
Data Bank established: 1990
Legislated Admissibility passed: no

MONTANA

First case: People v. Drummond. Sexual intercourse without consent allegedly committed by a State institution attendant against a developmentally disabled patient. The victim gave birth and DNA comparisons were done by Lifecodes. Defendant pleaded guilty. Jefferson County, 1989.
Data Bank established: no
Legislated Admissibility passed: no

NEVADA

Data Bank established: 1990
Legislated Admissibility passed: 1989

NEW HAMPSHIRE

First case: People v. Barnaby. DNA analysis admitted, according to State Attorney General's Office. Hillsborough County, 1989.
Appellate Decision: State v. Vandebogart, 1992. Reversed admission of DNA evidence and remanded case to trial court to determine if ceiling principle was acceptable, which the trial court did.
Data Bank established: no
Legislated Admissibility passed: no

NEW JERSEY

First case: People v. Beard. Nearly 3 months after being charged with murder, the defendant was released after a judge ruled that authorities arrested the wrong man. The primary suspect in a 1975 Georgia murder disappeared after the crime. Mistakenly, his cousin (the defendant in this case) was arrested. DNA tests conducted by Lifecodes proved the jailed man was not the father of a man known to be the son of the suspect. Union County, 1989.
Appellate Decision: State v. Williams, 1991. Affirmed the use of PCR.
Data Bank established: no
Legislated Admissibility passed: no

NEW MEXICO

First case: People v. Collins. A man once charged with killing his step-daughter was released from prison in October 1989 pending the outcome of DNA testing. Open murder charges against the defendant were dismissed in the interim. Santa Fe, 1989.
Appellate Decision: State v. Anderson, 1994. Reversed Court of Appeals ruling that DNA evidence, admitted by trial court, was inadmissible due to statistical methodology.
Data Bank established: no
Legislated Admissibility passed: no

NEW YORK

First case: People v. Zambrana, guilty of murder, New City, 1987.
Appellate Decision: People v. Wesley, 1994. Affirmed admissibility and statistical estimates.
Data Bank established: 1994
Legislated Admissibility passed: no

NORTH CAROLINA

First case: People v. Mills, guilty of murder, Salisbury, 1989.
Appellate Decision: State v. Pennington, 1990. Affirmed use of DNA evidence and statistics.
Data Bank established: 1993
Legislated Admissibility passed: no

NORTH DAKOTA

Data Bank established: no
Legislated Admissibility passed: no

OHIO

First case: People v. Dascenzo, guilty of aggravated murder, Montgomery County, 1988.
Appellate Decision: Ohio v. Penton, 1993. Affirmed PCR and reiterated relevancy as admissibility standard rather than Frye standard.
Data Bank established: no
Legislated Admissibility passed: no

OKLAHOMA

First case: People v. Hunt, first time Lifecodes testifies regarding DNA evidence in criminal case, defendant acquitted of murder, Norman, 1987.
Data Bank established: 1991
Legislated Admissibility passed: no

OREGON

First case: People v. Futch, DNA test results offered for admission at 7-month pretrial hearing, Clatsop County, 1989.
Appellate Decision: State v. Lyons, 1993. Affirmed use of DNA evidence and statistics.
Data Bank established: 1991
Legislated Admissibility passed: no

PENNSYLVANIA

First case: People v. Trubia, guilty of murder/rape, Lackawanna County, 1988.
Appellate Decision: Commonwealth v. Rogers, 1992. Affirmed DNA admissibility under Frye.
Data Bank established: no
Legislated Admissibility passed: no

RHODE ISLAND

First case: In re: Case involving rape of a nursing home resident. Juvenile admitted sufficient facts to establish the charge against him; sentenced to 3 years at a juvenile facility. 1989.
Data Bank established: no
Legislated Admissibility passed: no

SOUTH CAROLINA

First case: People v. Evans, guilty of rape/burglary, Charleston County, 1989.
Appellate Decision:
Data Bank established: no
Legislated Admissibility passed: no

SOUTH DAKOTA

First case: People v. Wimberly, guilty of rape, Meade County, 1989.
Appellate Decision: State v. Wimberly. Affirmed use of evidence and statistics.
Data Bank established: 1990
Legislated Admissibility passed: no

TENNESSEE

First case: FBI testimony in rape case in Blountville results in admission of DNA evidence, 1989, Trial pending.
Appellate Decision: People v. Harris, 1992. Affirmed admissibility and frequency estimate under both Frye and relevancy test.
Data Bank established: 1991
Legislated Admissibility passed: 1991

TEXAS

First case: People v. Trimboli, A DNA test that triple-murder defendant Ronald Trimboli had hoped would clear his name instead gave prosecutors additional evidence against him. Tests concluded that semen found on the bedspread where one of the three victims was raped matched a sample Trimboli had given for the test. Trimboli's two earlier trials for the three murders both ended in mistrials, first because of jury misconduct and later because a jury deadlocked, 6 to 6. The third trial resulted in a conviction on all three counts of murder. Tarrant County, test in 1988, convicted in 1989.
Appellate Decision: Kelly v. Texas, 1992. Affirmed DNA admissibility and concluded Frye was no longer part of Texas law.
Data Bank established: no
Legislated Admissibility passed: no

UTAH

First case: People v. Bickmore, DNA evidence admitted, mistrial declared on other grounds, Ogden, 1989.
Data Bank established: 1994
Legislated Admissibility passed: no

VERMONT

First case: United States v. Jakobetz. Admissibility hearing pending in rape case. Defense attorney has filed request that genetic evidence not be used in court. In August 1989, judge ruled that hair, blood, and saliva samples could be taken from defendant for testing. U.S. District Court, Burlington, 1989.
Data Bank established: no
Legislated Admissibility passed: no

VIRGINA

First case: People v. Reynolds, DNA evidence admitted in murder case, Henrico County, 1988.
Appellate Decision: Spencer v. Commonwealth, 1990. Affirmed use of DNA evidence.
Data Bank established: 1990
Legislated Admissibility passed: 1990

WASHINGTON

First case: People v. Young. DNA tests exclude Young, who had been identified by the victim as the rapist. Charges dropped, Snohomish County, 1989.
Appellate Decision: State v. Cauthron, 1993. Reversed trial courtís admission of DNA match without population statistics and remanded.
Data Bank established: 1990
Legislated Admissibility passed: no

WEST VIRGINIA

First case: People v. Ferrell, guilty of murder, Petersburg, 1989.
Data Bank established: 1993
Legislated Admissibility passed: no
Wisconsin
First case: People v. Banks, guilty of rape, Kenosha County, 1989.
Data Bank established: 1993
Legislated Admissibility passed: 1993

WYOMING

First case:
Appellate Decision: Springfield v. State, 1993. Affirmed use of DNA evidence and statistical calculations.
Data Bank established: no
Legislated Admissibility passed: no

MILITARY

First case: United States v. Scott. Rape case. Military judge approved request for DNA tests, but DNA in sample too degraded to perform the testing. U.S. Marine Corps, 1988.

Glossary

A. See adenine.

AABB. The American Association of Blood Banks Parentage Testing Committee, the voluntary inspection and certification organization for parentage testing laboratories located in Arlington, Virginia.

AAFS. The American Academy of Forensic Sciences, the primary national forensic scientific organization headquartered in Colorado Springs, Colorado. They hold an annual scientific meeting and publish the Journal of Forensic Science.

adenine. An organic base, one of the four monomers or building blocks from which DNA is made.

AFLP. Amplified fragment length polymorphism. A VNTR containing alleles generally less than one thousand base pairs in length that have been amplified using the PCR process. The length of the resulting DNA fragments, which are separated by electrophoresis, is determined by the PCR primers rather than the restriction enzyme site as is the case in RFLP. STRs are a class of AFLPs in which the repeat units are even smaller.

agarose. A jello like substance derived from seaweed that is used as a medium for the size separation of DNA and proteins by the process of electrophoresis.

allele frequency. The representation of a specific allele out of the total alleles observed at that locus.

allele. Alternative forms or versions of a gene. Each person has two alleles of every gene which may be the same or different. There may be a few or many alleles of a gene found in a population; some may be common others rare.

AMPFLP. See AFLP.

analytical gel. The final gel in an RFLP test and the one that will be used to make the Southern blot.

ASCLD-LAB. The American Society of Crime Laboratory Directors Laboratory Accreditation Board. The voluntary inspection and certification organization for crime laboratories. It is a separate organization from ASCLD itself.

ASHG. The American Society of Human Genetics.

ASHI. The American Society of Histocompatibility and Immunogenetics.

autorad. A film exposed by a radioactive tracer. In the case of forensic RFLP analysis the tracer is attached to a DNA probe which is in turn attached to a VNTR allele immobilized on a Southern blot.

autoradiogram. See autorad

autoradiograph. See autorad

autoradiography. See autorad

band. The exposed area on an autorad film that detects the presence of a particular DNA fragment.

bandshift. The phenomena in which identical DNA fragments will move through an electrophoresis gel at different rates because of contamination or alterations to the DNA itself. This phenomena is usually observed in forensic samples that are partially degraded.

base. The chemical units adenine (A), guanine (G), cytosine (C), and thymine (T) contained in DNA and that by virtue of their sequence determine the information content of the DNA.

base pair(ing). The complementary partnership of A with T and G with C that brings the two opposite strands of a DNA molecule together to form the double helix.

blot. See Southern blot.

C. See cytosine.

CAC. California Association of Criminalists.

CACLD. California Association of Crime Laboratory Directors.

CAP. College of American Pathologists. Supplies proficiency tests to forensic and parentage testing and medical laboratories.

ceiling principle. An extremely conservative method of calculating the estimated occurrence of DNA profiles in forensic samples. It's purpose is to compensate for any undetected substructure that may exist in the populations that have been sampled.

cell. The smallest unit of life that is capable of independent reproduction by the process of cell division. There are approximately 100 trillion cells in the human body almost all of which contain an identical complement of DNA known as the human genome.

chromosome. The units made up of proteins and DNA into which the DNA in cells is packaged. There are 23 pairs of chromosomes in each human cell.

cloning. The procedure for purifying and reproducing in the laboratory specific small identical DNA sequences.

CODIS. Combined DNA Identification System, the FBI's database of DNA profiles of convicted offenders supplied to them by the states.

complementarity. The characteristic of DNA resulting from the base pairing rules. If it is known that one strand has the sequence, GATC, then the sequence of the other complementary strand, CTAG, will also be known.

controls. Test samples for which the results are know. They are of two general types positive and negative. A positive control is used to confirm that the test worked correctly and a negative control to detect contamination. If a control test result does not meet specifications then the entire test can be rendered invalid.

CTS. Collaborative Testing Services, a commercial laboratory headquartered in Arlington, Virginia that supplies proficiency testing samples to forensic laboratories.

cytosine. An organic base, one of the four monomers or building blocks from which DNA is made.

degradation. The breaking down of DNA by biological or chemical processes. In the context of forensic science these processes are usually the result of cell death or exposure to the elements.

DNA. Deoxyribonucleic acid, the biological polymer that stores the genetic information in all free living organisms. Two linear molecules entwine to form the double helix.

DNA polymerase. An enzyme that produces or synthesizes DNA. These enzymes always use an existing DNA molecule as a template for producing a new strand of DNA.

DNA probe. A short piece of DNA made in the laboratory by chemical or biological means that can be labeled with a tracer and used to identify a specific gene. A specific gene is identified by a specific DNA probe.

DNA profiling or typing. A variety of DNA tests used by forensic scientists to aid in the identification of the individual source of evidence or to resolve a parentage question.

electrophoresis. The process of moving DNA or proteins through a sieving matrix that will separate them by size. This process is possible because most biological molecules have an electric charge and so will move in response to the electrical field that is applied to the separation matrix.

enzymes. Proteins that serve as catalysts for specific biological reactions. A catalyst is a substance that helps a chemical reaction occur. It remains unchanged itself and so is required in trace amounts. The two most commonly used in DNA testing are the restriction endonuclease Hae III and Taq DNA polymerase.

ethidium bromide (EtBr). A dye that stains DNA and is illuminated by ultraviolet or black light on a device called a transilluminator. It is used to visualize DNA in gels following electrophoresis and can be added to the DNA before or after electrophoresis. Its presence slightly alters the speed at which the DNA migrates through the gel. This fact has been the source of controversy in the past, but ample studies demonstrate that whether EtBr is added before or after electrophoresis does not significantly affect the results.

exclusion. In forensic and paternity testing the situation that exists when testing has demonstrated that a particular sample could not have come from an individual who was also tested or that the alleged father in a paternity case cannot be the father of the child.

forensic. Pertaining to, connected with, or used in courts of law.

forensic science. The application of scientific knowledge to questions of civil and criminal law, especially in court proceedings.

G. See guanine.

gel. A semi-solid matrix used in the electrophoretic separation of DNA and proteins. The two most commonly used in DNA testing are agarose and polyacrylamide.

gene. The fundamental unit of heredity, most commonly thought of as a stretch of DNA sequence that codes for a specific protein. The individually variable stretches of DNA that are examined by forensic scientists are not considered genes by strict definitions of the gene. For simplicity the term gene is used throughout this text when referring to these DNA fragments.

gene frequency. see allele frequency.

genome. The total genetic complement of an organism as defined by one copy of the total DNA found in each of its cells.

genotype. The genetic makeup of an individual consisting of both copies of the genetic information. The genotype is distinguished from the phenotype or physical characteristics of the individual. The pair of alleles at a locus or set of loci.

guanine. An organic base, one of the four monomers or building blocks from which DNA is made.

Hardy-Weinberg Principle. The concept that the presence of a particular allele at a locus has no predictive value as to what the other allele at that locus will be. It is a simple mathematical expression ($p^2+2pq+q^2=1$ where p and q are the allele frequencies of a pair of genes) based on the assumptions of a large population in which there is random mating. Population databases in use by forensic scientists must be tested to ensure that they obey this principle.

heredity. The phenomena whereby biological traits are passed from one generation to the next. Heredity results from parents passing genes to their offspring and is why related family members tend to have similar physical characteristics.

heterozygosity. In forensic science often used to describe the percentage of individuals in a population database who are heterozygotes.

heterozygote. An individual who has inherited and so carries different alleles of a gene.

HLA. Human leukocyte antigen, a substance found on the surface of most cells that differs from person to person. One of these, the DQA1 gene, is examined by the most widely used PCR based forensic DNA test.

homozygote. An individual who has identical alleles of a gene. An excess of homozygosity in a population database, according to the Hardy-Weinberg Principle, would indicate that there are problems with the data and that it should not be used.

hybridization. The joining together of complementary strands of DNA by the process of base pairing when the two strands are from different sources. For example, a DNA strand immobilized on a blot and its complementary radioactively labeled DNA probe.

hypervariable. A DNA locus that shows extremely high variation in people. Many alleles exist in the population.

inclusion. In forensic and paternity testing the situation that exists when testing has demonstrated that a particular individual belongs to the group of individuals who could be the source of the sample or in a paternity case the father of the child. They have not been excluded.

isotope. The radioactive form of an atom known as a radioisotope.

Kb. The abbreviation for kilobase or 1000 base pairs of DNA.

locus (pl. loci). A specific physical position on a chromosome at which a gene or gene pair resides. As scientists map genes to specific chromosomal locations they are registered with the Human Gene Mapping Workshop, assigned a name, and entered onto the genetic map of that chromosome.

linkage disequilibrium. A specific allele of one locus being found with a specific allele of another locus more often than would be expected by chance. Occurs when the two loci are close together on the same chromosome. They are then said to be linked because they will tend to be inherited together.

not accurate or precise [handwritten margin note]

Marker. 1. A genetic marker is a gene that has been mapped and can be identified. 2. A molecular weight marker is a DNA fragment of known size used as a comparison standard in estimating the size of a DNA fragment of unknown size.

membrane. The solid support, usually nylon membrane, to which the DNA is transferred and affixed during the Southern blotting process.

microgram. One millionth of a gram.

milliliter. One thousandth of a liter, the same as a cc or cubic centimeter.

mitochondria. Organelles that exist inside cells and that contain a small amount of DNA (16,000 bp). A small region of the mitochondrial DNA varies from person to person. Because a cell may contain many thousands of mitochondria there are correspondingly many more copies of the mitochondrial DNA available for testing.

molecular weight or size marker. See marker.

molecular biology. A modern branch of biology that attempts to explain biological phenomena in molecular terms. Most work in molecular biology is concerned with or uses genetic techniques.

molecule. The smallest physical unit of a chemical compound, the defined collection of atoms bound together in a specific fashion.

monomorphic probe. A DNA probe that will detect a DNA fragment that is the same size in everyone. Monomorphic probes are used to detect band shifting.

multilocus probe. The original Jefferys process of simultaneously detecting up to ten or fifteen genetic loci simultaneously. Because of technical problems with this method it has been supplanted in forensic science by the single locus probe method.

mutation. Any inheritable changes in the DNA sequence that occurs during reproduction or cell division.

nanogram. One billionth of a gram.

nucleotide. The monomer units that are used to make up the DNA molecule. Each has one of the four bases, A, G, T, or C attached to a sugar phosphate that forms the backbone of the DNA polymer.

obligate gene. In parentage testing the gene that must have been passed by the father to the child.

paternity index (PI). In parentage testing, the genetic odds in favor of paternity. When the alleged father has all the markers required to be the father, he cannot be excluded from paternity. The paternity index is the ratio between the chance that the alleged father may pass the obligatory gene compared to the chance that a random man of the same race may pass the obligatory gene.

PCR. See polymerase chain reaction.

phenotype. The physical characteristics of an organism resulting from the interaction of their genotype with the environment.

Polymerase chain reaction. An in vitro method for reproducing DNA in the laboratory. Many millions of copies of a defined short sequence can be made in a short time. Repeated cycling of the reaction allows the new DNA to increase in a geometric fashion.

polymorphic locus. A genetic locus for which there are many alleles in existence. The loci used in forensic science are the most polymorphic known.

population. A defined group of individuals for which databases of gene frequencies are collected by sampling members of the population. In forensic science population databases are collected and maintained by major racial or ethnic group.

population substructure. The hypothesis that within the major population groups there exist subgroups whose allele frequency patterns would differ from the parent population to such an extent that the database would not be suitable for forensic use. This phenomena is described by the Wahlund principle.

primer. A short piece of DNA, usually synthetic, that defines the specific site on a DNA molecule for a DNA polymerase to start making new DNA. An essential ingredient in the PCR reaction mix.

probability of paternity. A statistic, expressed as a percentage, incorporating the genetic evidence (paternity index) and the non-genetic evidence (prior chance), which compares the likelihood the tested man may pass the required genes to the likelihood that an untested random man of the same race may pass these genes. This value may approach, but never reach, 100%. Also know as the W value.

product rule. The concept from elementary probability theory that allows the frequency of occurrence of independent events to be multiplied together to estimate how often they would occur together.

proficiency tests. Testing of laboratory personnel performed as part of a quality assurance program. Samples of known composition are supplied to analysts by outside agencies or laboratory management as a way of evaluating and maintaining performance standards.

protein. A biological polymer made up of amino acids whose structure is coded for by the DNA. Proteins are the primary structural, functional and regulatory molecules of the body. Enzymes are a major class of proteins.

protocol. Laboratory procedures manual.

quality assurance. Externally administered programs that are design to assess and maintain a minimum level of laboratory performance. It includes laboratory inspection and accreditation, personnel training, examination and certification, regular proficiency testing and the maintenance of a quality control program.

quality control. Systematic regular activities for verifying and maintaining a specified level of quality in a product or process. It includes careful planning, regular documentation, continued inspection and measurement and the implementation of corrective action when necessary.

replication. The enzymatic process of making new DNA based on the use of use of an existing strand of DNA as a template. The enzymes that perform this process require a primer, a short piece of DNA complementary to the template that defines the base at which the replication will start and that will become part of the newly synthesized DNA.

restriction enzymes (RE), restriction endonucleases. A class of enzymes obtained from microorganisms that cut the DNA strands at specific four to twelve base pair sequences. There are over one hundred restriction enzymes commercially available each having a different recognition site. In forensic science the most commonly used RE is called Hae III although there are some labs who still use Hinf I or Pst I.

RE test gel. A gel used to analyze DNA that has been cut by a restriction enzyme (RE) to ensure that the cutting of the DNA has been complete. Sometimes contaminants in forensic samples will inhibit the action of the enzyme and prevent it from cutting the DNA.

restriction fragment length polymorphism (RFLP). Variations in the length of a DNA restriction fragment caused by the presence of a polymorphic locus within the fragment. Analysis of RFLPs by the Southern blotting method is the most common and definitive forensic DNA test.

RNA ribonucleic acid. A nucleic acid polymer similar to DNA and used to translate the genetic code into a form useful by the cells.

scanner. Common term for the computer driven video devices used to electronically estimate the sizes of DNA restriction fragments detected in a forensic RFLP test.

serology. In forensic science the study of body fluids and body fluid stains. Forensic DNA analysis is generally performed by specially trained forensic serologists.

single locus probe. The currently used practice in forensic DNA analysis of detecting the restriction fragments in a DNA profile one locus at a time.

Southern blotting. The technique of transferring DNA fragments in a gel to a solid support such as a sheet of nylon. The resulting sheet of nylon with the DNA permanently affixed to it is referred to as the blot.

STR. Short tandem repeat see AFLP.

T. See thymine.

Taq DNA polymerase. The heat stable DNA polymerase used in the PCR reaction.

thymine. An organic base, one of the four monomers or building blocks from which DNA is made.

variable number of tandem repeat (VNTR). The class of genetic loci most commonly used in forensic DNA analysis. They are composed of 9 to 75 base pair sequences that are repeated different numbers of times in different people. Hence, the physical length of the DNA molecule at these loci will vary from person to person.

yield gel. A gel run for the purpose of assessing the quantity and quality of the DNA extracted from a sample.

Recommended Resources

BASIC DOCUMENTS

National Research Council, *DNA Technology in Forensic Science*. Washington, DC: National Academy Press, 1992.

U.S. Congress Office of Technology Assessment, *Genetic Witness: Forensic Uses of DNA Tests*. Washington, DC: U.S. Government Printing Office, 1990.

Court Documents in:

New York v. Castro

U.S. v. Yee

U.S. v. Porter

Florida v. Andrews

Virginia v. Spencer

California v. Axell

California v. Barney & Howard

California v. Soto

DNA SCIENCE AND TECHNOLOGY

Burgoyne, L. A., Robertson, J., Ross, A. M., eds. *DNA in Forensic Science: Theory, Techniques and Applications*. West Sussex, England: Ellis Horwood Limited, 1990.

Chakraborty, R., Kidd, K. "The Utility of DNA Typing in Forensic Work," *Science*, Vol. 254, 1991: 1735.

Farley, M. A., Harrington, J. J., eds. *Forensic DNA Technology*. Chelsea, MI: Lewis Publishers, Inc., 1991.

Frank-Kamenetskii, M. D. *Unraveling DNA*. New York, NY: VCH Publishers, Inc., 1993.

Hartl, D., Lewontin, R. "Population Genetics in Forensic DNA Typing," *Science*, Vol. 254, 1991: 1745.

Herrera, R. J., Tracey, M. J. "DNA Fingerprinting: Basic Techniqes, Problems, and Solutions," *Journal of Criminal Justice*, May-Jun., 1992: 237.

Judson, H. F. *The Eighth Day of Creation*. New York, NY: Simon and Schuster, 1979.

King, R. C. *A Dictionary of Genetics*. New York, NY: Oxford University Press, 1990.

Kirby, L. T. *DNA Fingerprinting, An Introduction*. New York, NY: Stockton Press.

Mange, A. P., Mange, E. J. *Basic Human Genetics*. Sunderland, MA: Sinauer Associates, Inc., 1990.

Pena, S. D., ed. *DNA Fingerprinting: State of the Science*. Boston, MA: Basel, 1993.

Promega. International Symposium on Human Identification. *Conference Proceedings*, 1989-1994.

Roeder, K. "DNA Fingerprinting: A Review of the Controversy," *Statistical Science*, Vol. 9, No. 2, 1994: 22.

Starrs, J. E. "DNA in the Journals: The Good, the Bad and the Maladroit." *Scientific Sleuthing Newsletter*, Vol. 12, No. 3.

Watson, J. D. *The Double Helix*. New York, NY: W. W. Norton & Company, 1980.

Zurer, Pamela. "DNA Profiling Fast Becoming Accepted Tool For Identification," *Chemical and Engineering News* October 10, 1994: 8.

THE DNA WAR AND THE LAW

Anderson, A. "DNA Fingerprinting on Trial," *Nature*, Vol. 342, 1989: 844.

Anderson, C. "DNA Fingerprinting Discord," *Nature*, Vol. 354, 1991: 500.

Anon. "The FBI's Responses to Recommendations by the NRC's Committee on DNA Technology in Forensic Science": *Crime Laboratory Digest*, Vol. 19, July 1992

Billings, P. R., ed. *DNA on Trial: Genetic Identification and Criminal Justice*. U.S.A: Cold Springs Harbor Laboratory Press, 1992.

Brown, W. "Doubts Over DNA Evidence Exaggerated," *New Scientist*, Jan. 23, 1993: 6.

Budowle, B., Lander, E. S. "DNA Fingerprinting Dispute Laid to Rest," *Nature*, Vol. 371, Oct. 27, 1994: 735.

Colman, N., Neufeld, P. "When Science Takes the Witness Stand," *Scientific American*, Vol. 262, 1990: 46.

Flannery, I. M. "Frye or Frye Not: Should the Reliability of DNA Evidence be a Question of Weight or Admissibility?" *American Criminal Law Review*, Fall 1992: 161.

Ford, S., Thompson, W. A. "DNA Testing: Debate Update," *Trial*, April 1992: 52.

Ford, S., Thompson, W. A. "Is DNA Fingerprinting Ready for Court?" *New Scientist*, Vol. 125, 1990: 38.

Giannelli, P. C. "The Admissibility of Novel Scientific Evidence: Frye v. United States, a Half-Century Later," *Columbia Law Review*, Vol. 80: 1198.

Harmon, R. "Staying Dumb About DNA," *The Recorder*, Jul. 18, 1994: 8.

Humes, E. "DNA War," *L.A. Times Magazine*, Nov. 29, 1992: 29.

Lander, E. S., "DNA Fingerprinting on Trial," *Nature*, Vol. 339, 1989: 501.

Lewis, R. "DNA Fingerprints: Witness for the Prosecution," *Discover*, June 1988: 44.

MacKnight, K. T. "The Polymerase Chain Reaction (PCR): The Second Generation of DNA Analysis Methods Takes the Stand," *Santa Clara Computer and High Technology Law Journal*, Vol. 9, No. 1, 1993: 288.

Marx, J. L., "DNA Fingerprinting Takes the Witness Stand," *Science*, Vol. 240, 1988: 1616.

Moss, D. C. "DNA-The New Fingerprints," *American Bar Association Journal*, May 1, 1988: 66.

Roberts, L. "Fight Erupts Over DNA Fingerprinting," *Science*, Vol. 254, 1991: 1721.

Roberts, L. "Science in Court: A Culture Clash," *Science*, Vol. 257, 1992: 732.

Sherman, R. "DNA Unraveling," *National Law Journal*, Feb. 1, 1991: 1.

Thompson, W. A. "Evaluating the Admissibility of New Genetic Identification Tests: Lessons From the DNA War," *The Journal of Criminal Law & Criminology*, Vol. 84, No. 1, 1993: 22.

Weiss, R. "DNA Takes the Stand," *Science News*, Jul. 29, 1989: 74.

CRIME AND FORENSICS

Saferstein, R. *Criminalistics:* Fourth Edition. Englewood Cliffs, NJ: Prentice Hall, 1990.

Wambaugh, J. *The Blooding*. New York, NY: William Morrow Co., 1989.

NOTES

NOTES

NOTES

NOTES

THE AUTHORS

Howard C. Coleman is the president and chairman of GeneLex Corporation, the Seattle-based DNA laboratory he founded in 1987. After reading the first reports of "DNA fingerprinting" in British scholarly journals in 1985, Coleman ended his graduate studies in molecular biology to establish a forensic and paternity DNA testing laboratory. GeneLex has become a nationally recognized pioneer in the field. The pH30 testing probe developed by GeneLex is acknowledged to be an industry standard.

Coleman has appeared as an expert witness for both the defense and prosecution in numerous court cases, and has spoken scores of times to forensic science, law, and student groups. He is the author of several scholarly papers on forensic DNA analysis, has patented a DNA testing device, and was the author of a National Institute of Justice grant in 1987 for the forensic applications of DNA methods. This year he was elected a director of the Human Identity Trade Association and has been a guest on Larry King Live, Rivera Live, and the CNN morning news among others. He is currently at work with Eric Swenson on *Silent Witness: DNA and Criminal Justice in America*, a full-length study of the "DNA Wars" of which the Simpson case may be the last major battle.

Eric D. Swenson, in the last decade, has written or co-authored five books including *The Complete Baseball Player*, with Dave Winfield (Avon 1990). He has also written more than 80 magazine articles and broadcast 50 commentaries for National Public Radio affiliates in the Northwest. Swenson has taught advanced writing about science and technology, technical writing, and other writing classes at several colleges and universities, including Oregon State University and the University of Washington.

ORDER FORM

Please send the following:

QTY.	TITLE	PRICE	TOTAL
	DNA in the Courtroom... **A Trial Watcher's Guide** *By Howard Coleman & Eric Swenson* DNA in the Courtroom provides the media, attorneys and law enforcement with a comprehensive, succinct guide to the scientific, and legal issues surrounding forensic DNA testing.	$12.95	
	Forensic DNA Laboratory Video Tour A tour of the GeneLex laboratory from evidence receipt and screening through generation of reports. Shows all the steps involved in RFLP and PCR DNA testing methods. 9 minutes.	$24.95	
	DNA Analysis...35mm slide set This slide set, containing over two dozen slides, can be used both as a teaching and training aid and as a testimony/ trial tool. The slides take the audience from basic fertilization to DNA analysis methods to the most recent DNA developments.	$95.00	
	DNA Demonstration Beads "Presley" DNA demonstration beads can be used in the courtroom or the classroom to show how DNA varies from person to person.	$24.95	

* Shipping: $3.50 for first book
or video, .75¢ for each additional
book or video. Airmail: $5.50.

TOTAL	
Washington residents add 8.2% sales tax	
* Shipping and Handling	
GRAND TOTAL	

Please fill in:

Name _____

Address _____

City _____ State _____ Zip _____

Phone (_____) _____ Occupation _____

Payment method: ☐ Check   ☐ Credit Card (☐ VISA ☐ Mastercard)

Card # _____

Name on card _____ Exp. date _____

Signature _____

To Order by Phone Call Toll Free:
1-800-523-3080
(Please have your VISA or Mastercard ready)

Fax to: **1-206-382-6277**

Mail to: **GeneLex Corporation**
Attn: Book Order Dept.
2203 Airport Way South, Suite 350
Seattle, WA 98134